~1000~
English Idioms

Explained

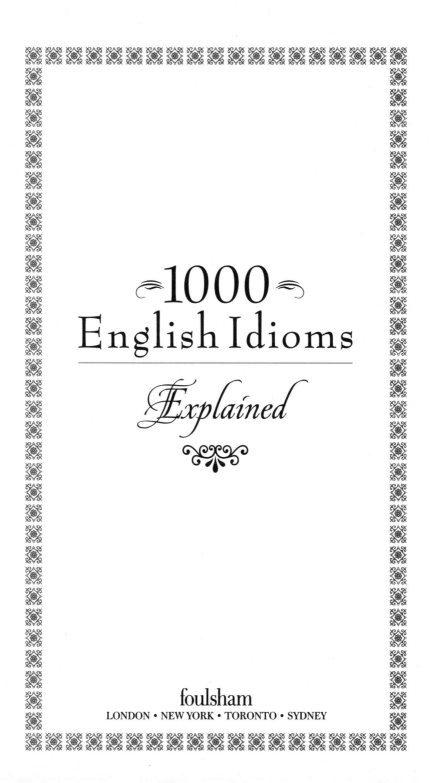

∞1000∞
English Idioms
Explained

foulsham
LONDON • NEW YORK • TORONTO • SYDNEY

foulsham

The Publishing House, Bennetts Close, Cippenham,
Slough, Berkshire, SL1 5AP, England

Foulsham books can be found in all good bookshops and direct from
www.foulsham.com

ISBN: 978-0-572-03390-3

Copyright © 2007 W. Foulsham & Co. Ltd

Cover photograph © Mary Evans Picture Library

A CIP record for this book is available from the British Library

Printed in Great Britain by Creative Print and Design (Wales), Ebbw Vale

Introduction

Have you ever told your child to stop being stroppy? Do you sometimes want to call a spade a spade, but hesitate because it may cause offence? What does 'all grist to the mill' mean – and why do your grandparents have antimacassars on their sofa? Are flotsam and jetsam the same thing? Are kith and kin?

English is a fascinating language and it is developing all the time. Our communication with others is vastly enriched by the expressions we use, making what we say more concise, more amusing and more interesting. English idiom has many diverse sources, including the Bible and the Qu'ran, folk tales, town and country life, other languages, warfare, politics and sport. It is only to be expected that Britain, being an island, should have generated expressions related to a seafaring life, but it is surprising just how many there are and that they are still so current.

In this book you will find 1000 English idioms, with an explanation of how they entered the language and what we mean when we use them. Some are many hundreds of years old; others have come into being only very recently. Most are likely to be familiar and ones you use almost without thinking; but there may be some that are new to you and, hopefully, now you have found them you will take them on board – and there's another marine expression! – and will wonder how you ever managed to say exactly what you wanted to say without them.

A-1

Why do we use 'A-1' to mean 'the very best'?

We have borrowed this description from the marine insurance firms of London. When they founded the association later to become known as 'Lloyd's', they also started a register of ships and shipping in which the condition of the ships and their cargo was noted. The ships were graded by letter, the cargoes by number. 'A' meant the ship itself was perfect, '1' that the cargo was likewise perfect.

Abacus

Where did we get the name 'abacus' for the 'calculator' used by the Chinese and others?

The device takes its name from the ancient Phoenician word *abak* meaning 'dust'; the mathematicians of that day used to cover the top surfaces of tables with dust in order to draw their diagrams and work out their problems.

About face

What do we mean when we say someone's done an 'about face'?

This comes from the 180-degree turn a soldier makes on the parade ground; obviously, once he has performed the command, he will be facing in the opposite direction. The general meaning of this term is changing your mind completely.

Above board

Why is an honest person said to be 'above board'?

Because cardsharps and magicians place their hands under the 'board' or table, to prepare their tricks and stack the deck. If they keep their hands above the board they can be presumed − not always correctly − to be performing without trickery.

Abracadabra
Where did the magic word 'abracadabra' come from?
This cabalistic word, said to have been the name of the supreme deity of the Assyrians, was recommended by Quintus Severus Sammonicus as a charm against various ailments – including fever and toothache – if written on a piece of paper, hung round the neck, in this pyramid form:

ABRACADABRA
ABRACADABR
ABRACADAB
ABRACADA
ABRACAD
ABRACA
ABRAC
ABRA
ABR
AB
A

Abraham's bosom
Why are good people who have died supposed to rest in, or on, 'Abraham's bosom'?
Because it indicates the reward of the holy. It was the custom among the ancients for a person to allow a dear friend to recline on his chest while eating. Only the righteous dead, who have gone to heaven and been welcomed by Abraham, could hope to recline on his bosom.

Accost
Why is it that a person who speaks to you without introduction is said to 'accost' you?
It is because he usually sidles up to you. The Latin word for 'side' is *costa* – and 'accost' literally means 'at the side'.

Achilles' heel
Why do we use the phrase 'Achilles' heel' to refer to a person's vulnerable spot?
In Greek mythology, Thetis, the mother of Achilles, dipped him into the River Styx to make him invulnerable. Because she held him by his heel, this became his one vulnerable spot. Achilles died of a wound received from an arrow shot into his heel.

Acid test
Which acid was used in the 'acid test'?
A mixture of nitric acid and hydrochloric acid. Because it dissolves gold, it was used to test whether gold offered for sale was genuine. The 'acid test' itself was used from the Middle Ages, but now the phrase is applied to any decisive test to prove the worth or reliability of something or someone.

Acre

How did we get 'acre' as a measure of land?

The word 'acre' originally meant a field – any field. In the reign of Edward I of England, an exact definition was set as the amount of land a team of oxen could plough in a day – 40 poles long by 4 broad, or 4,840 square yards.

Acrobat

Where did the word 'acrobat' come from?

It is a Greek word, which literally (and succinctly) means 'one who goes about on the tips of his toes and fingers'.

Across the board

What do we mean when we say that a something applies 'across the board'?

When a decision is made 'across the board', the same conditions will be applied to everyone or everything. The expression is of American origin and comes from a horse-racing bet in which equal amounts are staked on a horse to come in first, second or third. The 'board' itself was the blackboard on which bookmakers chalked up the odds for each horse in each race.

Adam's apple

How did the larynx come to be called the 'Adam's apple'?

The term is an allusion to the story of the Garden of Eden. Supposedly, a piece of the forbidden fruit stuck in Adam's throat and created his 'Adam's apple' – women have them too, though they are usually smaller.

Addled

How did 'addled' come to mean a person lacking in wit?

'Addle' comes from the Anglo-Saxon word for 'filth' – *adela*. An addled egg is a rotten egg – one that will not hatch and so perform its normal function. From an addled egg we get the idea of a person who is unable to perform normal functions being 'addled'.

Admiral

Where did we get the word 'admiral'?

From the Arabians. The Arabian *amir* means 'ruler' or 'commander' and *bahr* means 'sea'. An Arabian sea commander was called an *amir al bahr* or 'ruler of the sea'.

Adroit

Why does 'adroit' mean an adept and agile person?

Because this word – which comes from the French *à droit* – means 'to the right'. The French – and most other people – once presumed that only a right-handed person could be skilful.

Against the grain

What is the reason we say that something we do not like goes 'against the grain'?

When a carpenter uses his plane against the grain of the wood, he roughens the surface instead of smoothing it. So, too, anything that 'goes against the grain' irritates us.

Agony column

Why are the personal problems published in newspapers and magazines called the 'agony column'?

The second column of the first page of *The Times* was once devoted to personal advertisements. They were so often full of cries of anguish from aching hearts that it acquired the name 'agony column'.

Ahead of the pack

How did 'ahead of the pack' come to mean that you have the advantage?

From the behaviour of animals that hunt in packs. The first one to a kill gets the best meat so, if you are ahead of the pack, you have the advantage over your rivals.

Albatross round your neck

Where does having an 'albatross round your neck' originate?

Seeing an albatrosses during a voyage was considered a lucky omen by sailors. If a sailor killed one, it was tied round his neck as a punishment. So, if you have an insuperable problem of your own making, you have an 'albatross round your neck'.

Album

What was an 'album' originally?

A table with a white top on which were kept the names of Roman officials and accounts of public proceedings, which was prominently displayed in a public place. The word comes from the Latin *albus*, meaning 'white'. The British adopted the term during the Middle Ages and used it to signify a register or list of persons. From this, the word 'album' acquired its present meaning.

Alcohol

Has 'alcohol' always meant spirits?

No, 'alcohol' originally meant 'eye paint'. The ancient Egyptians – and later the Arabians – used a fine black powder for tinting the eyelids. The Arabian name for this was *al koh'l* and from this any fine powder acquired the name. Finally the vinous spirits extracted by means of a charcoal filter came to be called 'alcohol'.

Alexander's beard

How did we come to swear by 'Alexander's beard'?

Alexander the Great of Macedon disliked hairy faces. He himself shaved and he ordered all his men to shave likewise – lest an enemy grab one by the beard and lop his head off. Therefore, to 'swear by Alexander's beard' is to swear by nothing at all.

Alimony
Why is payment to a divorcée called 'alimony'?
Because it is her (or, indeed, his) bread and butter. The word comes from the Latin *alimonia* meaning 'nourishment'.

Alive and kicking
What is the derivation of the description 'alive and kicking'?
The expression originated in around 1850 and was used by fishmongers to convince customers of the freshness of their wares. The current use – to describe something or someone that is still vigorous despite opinions to the contrary – originated in the 1960s and was used as a denial of a reported death.

All bells and whistles
Is it good to buy a gadget with 'all bells and whistles'?
Not necessarily. The term was originally coined as a disapproving description of a device laden with features included more for commercial appeal than necessity. More recently it has been used positively, perhaps in the product's own advertising literature – for instance for the mobile phones so technologically advanced they are practically computers.

All dressed up and nowhere to go
When did the saying 'all dressed up and nowhere to go' originate?
In 1916, from the popular song 'When You're All Dressed Up and Nowhere To Go' by B.H. Burt. You would use the expression if you were all ready and waiting for something exciting to happen, but were then disappointed by the plans falling apart.

All Greek to me
Why do I say something incomprehensible is 'all Greek to me'?
The expression derives from Shakespeare's *Julius Caesar*, when Casca says he has not understood a speech made by Cicero in Greek.

All grist to the mill
What do we mean when we say 'all grist to the mill'?
That everything is useful towards achieving the desired outcome. It was first cited in *The Sermons of J. Calvin upon Deuteronomie* in 1583: 'There is no lykelihoode that those thinges will bring gryst to the mill.' 'Grist' is the unprocessed corn brought to the mill to grind into flour.

All my eye and Betty Martin
Why do we use the expression 'all my eye and Betty Martin' to mean nonsense?
The expression owes its popularity to a story once in wide circulation. A British sailor went into a foreign church where he heard the priest uttering these words: *Ah, mihi, beate Martine* (Ah, grant me, Blessed Martin). In telling of his experience the sailor said: 'And all the sense the fellow ever made was when he said "All my eye and Betty Martin".'

All over bar the shouting

Why do we say a foregone conclusion is 'all over bar the shouting'?

It comes from sports, when the outcome of a contest or game was so certain even before it happened, that it might as well not take place – except for the noisy post-game celebrations.

All present and correct

Does 'all present and correct' have a military origin?

Yes. It's an expression used by a sergeant-major at an inspection of the troops. It is now used light-heartedly to mean 'here, ready and waiting'.

All in the same boat

How did 'all in the same boat' come to mean equality of opportunity – or lack of it?

The allusion is to a shipwreck. When a ship is wrecked and has to be abandoned, all class distinctions must be abandoned as well. Each person must accept and share the common fate – they're 'all in the same boat'.

All singing, all dancing

Can something that is 'all singing, all dancing' do absolutely everything?

It means that now, but the description initially came from posters advertising the 1929 *Broadway Melody* and was intended to suggest the vitality and excitement of what was the first ever film musical. Now it is often applied to top-of-the-range items such as computers and cars to draw attention to their distinctive features.

All and sundry

What do we mean by 'all and sundry'?

This simply means 'everyone'. The expression comes from fourteenth-century legal jargon designed to make sure every option was covered.

All systems go

When was 'all systems go' first said to mean that everything is ready for immediate action?

In the 1960s by NASA, during the heyday of space flight. It referred to the launching of missiles and space vehicles.

All that glitters is not gold

Was Shakespeare the creator of the expression 'all that glitters is not gold'?

No, there is an earlier occurrence. The twelfth-century French theologian Alain de Lille wrote: 'Do not hold everything gold that shines like gold.' However, most of us know the expression from Shakespeare's *The Merchant of Venice*, in which Portia's suitors must choose in which of three caskets – gold, silver or lead – her father has hidden her portrait. The warning 'all that glitters is not gold' is found inside the gold casket: the portrait is, of course, inside the lead casket. We use this expression to advise people that the showiest article may not necessarily be the most valuable.

Allspice
Does the word 'allspice' mean the seasoning is a combination of all seasonings?
No. Allspice is a dried and ground variety of pimiento. It gets its name, however, from the fact that it tastes like a mixture of ground nutmeg, cloves and cinnamon.

Alma mater
Why do we call the college we attend our 'alma mater'?
Because this Latin phrase literally means 'nursing mother' or 'nourishing mother'. The term is applied to colleges and other institutions of learning, as they are supposed to nourish the minds of their students.

Aloof
Where does the word 'aloof' get its meaning?
From sailing. A strong onshore breeze may blow a sailing ship on to coastal rocks. To keep clear, the helmsman must hold the vessel into the wind. The nautical term 'luff' means 'to the windward'. Thus to 'hold a-luff' – or, as we now say, 'aloof' – means to keep clear.

Alphabet
Why do we call our ABCs the 'alphabet'?
The Greek alphabet begins with the letters *alpha* and *beta* – hence 'alphabet'. Likewise, 'abecederia', a name for school primers, takes its name from the first four letters of the alphabet.

Also ran
How did a nonentity come to be called an 'also ran'?
The term comes from the sporting pages of newspapers. In a horse race those entries that do not finish near the front are listed under the terse heading 'also ran'.

Amazon
Who gave the name 'Amazon' to strong, masculine women?
The Greeks. The word literally means 'without a breast'. It refers to the Grecian story of a nation of warlike women in Asia Minor. These women were such determined warriors that they burned off their right breasts in order to better draw a bow.

Ambition
What did the word 'ambition' originally mean?
Literally 'go-getting'. The ancient Romans used the world *ambitio* to describe a candidate's 'going about for votes'.

Ambulance

Why do we call the vehicle for moving stretcher cases an 'ambulance' when walking cases are 'ambulant'?

Because the ambulance once brought the hospital to the patient. The French devised the term and applied it to their early field hospitals, which they called *hôpitals ambulants*. From this, the name 'ambulance' was applied to the vehicle – and it kept the name when it reversed the process and started bringing patients to hospital.

Amen

What is the real meaning of 'amen'?

'Amen' is generally accepted as meaning 'so be it'. But in the Hebrew language, from which it comes, *amen* literally means 'truly'. When we use the word at the end of a prayer or hymn, we assert its truth and sincerity. 'Amen' is also the last word in the Bible.

Amen Corner

How did the Amen Corner get its name?

It started in England. Today the term refers to the section of a revival meeting where the approving sit and signify their approval by interjecting frequent 'amens'. It originally meant the end of a street in London. On Corpus Christi Day, the priests went in procession to St Paul's Cathedral – reciting the Lord's Prayer in Latin as they walked along. The prayer begins *Pater Noster* – and so the street was called 'Paternoster Row'. When they got to the end of the prayer they were at the end of the street and they turned the corner – 'Amen Corner'. As the priests turned down the lane they began chanting their *Ave Maria* or 'Hail Mary' – and so the lane was called 'Ave Maria Lane'.

American dream

What do we mean by the expression 'the American dream'?

The early European settlers in America believed that by hard work, courage and resolve anyone could achieve prosperity. This conviction was passed on to subsequent generations and is held by many in the United States today – though what actually constitutes the American dream is the subject of constant discussion and revision.

Amethyst

What is the meaning of the word 'amethyst'?

Literally, 'not intoxicating'. The word is Greek and the Greeks believed that wine drunk from an amethyst cup was not intoxicating. Indeed, just wearing a ring with this stone in it was considered sufficient protection.

Ampersand
Why do we call the '&' sign an 'ampersand'?
The old hornbooks from which children once learned their letters listed the letters of the alphabet – and ended this list with '&'. The children were taught their letters by being made to recite: 'A by itself A', 'B by itself B', and so on. However, they often used the Latin form 'A *per se* A', 'B *per se* B', and so on. When they came to the sign for 'and' they said: 'And *per se* And' – and this ultimately became 'ampersand'. The sign '&' is merely a monogram of the Latin word for 'and' – *et*.

Analyse
What is the original meaning of 'analyse'?
The word, which comes to us from the Greek, literally means 'to loosen up'. The primitive method of gathering gold dust was 'to loosen up' the earth and then toss it from a shallow pan up into the air. Just as tossing a handful of grain into the air winnows out the chaff, so the breeze would blow away the earth – and only gold would fall back into the pan.

Angry young man
Who was the original 'angry young man'?
The disaffected Jimmy Porter in John Osborne's 1956 play *Look Back in Anger*. The harsh realism of the play broke new theatrical ground in its contrast to the lightly entertaining productions of earlier generations.

Antimacassar
Why are the little cloth panels laid on the back of a chair called 'antimacassars'?
In the early part of the nineteenth century, it was the custom for men to oil their hair. The most popular hair oil was known as 'Oil of Macassar'. Careful housekeepers found that a piece of cloth placed on the chair where the head rested afforded protection against oil spots on the upholstery – hence the name 'antimacassar' for a chair doily.

Apex
Why is the topmost part of something called its 'apex'?
The priests of ancient Rome wore a close-fitting cap, which had a pointed olive wood spike on top called an *apex*. It was the highest piece of the priest's garb, and today we call the highest spot of anything the 'apex'.

Apple of discord
Does the 'apple of discord' refer to the apple eaten by Adam and Eve?
No. The allusion comes from Greek mythology. At the marriage of Thetis and Peleus, Discord threw a golden apple on the table, saying that it was for the most beautiful goddess there. Hera, Athene and Aphrodite all claimed it. Paris was called upon to settle the point and decided in favour of Aphrodite. According to the story, the resulting dispute between the three goddesses caused the Trojan War.

Apple of the eye
Why is a loved one called the 'apple of the eye'?
The 'apple of the eye' is the pupil. 'Apple' is probably a corruption of 'pupil' – as people originally thought the pupil of the eye was a little round ball like an apple. In any event, the allusion is to the image of the adored person so filling the pupil of the eye that nothing else can be seen.

Apple jack
How did cider get the name 'apple jack'?
It was once supposed that cider did not ripen and become properly potent until St John's Day – 24 June – hence the common names 'apple john' and 'apple jack'.

Apple pie order
Why do we use the phrase 'apple pie order' to mean something extremely neat and orderly?
Although sliced apples placed neatly one upon the other produce a neat geometric pattern, the phrase comes from the French *nappes pliées*, meaning 'folded linen'.

April fools' day
How did 1 April come to be called 'April fools' day'?
Up until 1564, New Year's Day in France was 25 March; but since it so often fell during Holy Week, the Church generally postponed its celebration to 1 April. Then New Year's Day was officially changed to 1 January – but many people still called out New Year's greetings to their friends on 1 April. Such persons were therefore 'April fools'; or, as the French say, *poissons d'avril* – 'April fish'.

Argus–eyed
Why do we use the expression 'Argus-eyed' to describe a vigilant observer?
Because the mythical Argus had a hundred eyes with which to observe things. In the story, Argus was set to watch over the heifer Io by Juno – who suspected her husband Mercury of being too fond of the calf. Mercury finally succeeded in putting all the eyes of Argus to sleep and then slew him. Whereupon, Juno changed Argus into a peacock – and that is how it happens that the peacock has a hundred 'eyes' in its tail.

Armed to the teeth
What do we mean by the expression 'armed to the teeth'?
Fourteenth–century warriors were often so laden with powerful weapons that sometimes they would have to carry one in their teeth. We say this of someone who is completely prepared and equipped for a confrontation.

Assassin
How did an 'assassin' get that name?
In the year 1090 AD Hasan ibn-al-Sabbah formed a secret Mohammedan sect in Persia, which during the Crusades terrorised the Christians by its systematic secret murders. These murders were committed by members of the band while under the influence of hashish – and the Arabian word for a hashish eater is *hashshashin*. The ruler of this order of Assassins had absolute power over all its members and was called 'The Old Man of the Mountain' – possibly from the fact that he made his headquarters on Mount Lebanon.

At each other's throats
Why do we say two people arguing are 'at each other's throats'?
Fighting dogs are bred to attack their prey's neck and clamp their jaws shut so they can hang on for as long as necessary until the prey is dead. People who are at each other's throats are fighting and neither has any intention of giving way.

At the end of your tether
Why are you 'at the end of your tether' when your patience is exhausted?
This expression relates to a tethered animal. It can roam so far, but no further – as would be the case of a person whose patience had been tried to its very limits.

At full tilt
Do we say something is going 'at full tilt' because it's so fast it might lean and fall over?
No. 'Tilt' is from the Old English *tealt* or *tylte*. Tilting was the early name for jousting in Medieval England, a sport involving two horseback knights charging at each other with lances. The winner was the knight who knocked the other off his horse. Nowadays something 'at full tilt' is going at top speed with maximum energy.

At one fell swoop
Where did the expression 'at one fell swoop' originate?
In Shakespeare's *Macbeth*. These are the words of the heartbroken Macduff on hearing of the mass murder of his wife and children. A 'swoop' is a sudden descent like a bird of prey on to its victim; 'fell' is from the Old French word *fel*, meaning 'merciless'. In modern use we say this just to mean 'all at once', forgetting the phrase's tragic genesis.

Auld Lang Syne
Where do we get the expression 'auld lang syne'?
It's a Scottish phrase that literally means 'old long since' – in other words, the 'olden times'. The composer and author of the song 'Auld Lang Syne' are unknown, though it is often attributed to Robert Burns, who heard an old man singing it and took it down.

Avoid like the plague

How long has the expression 'avoid like the plague' been in use?

Since the fourth century, when the plague was rampant. The only way to avoid its then inevitably fatal outcome was to take all measures not to contract it in the first place. The expression is therefore self-explanatory.

AWOL

What do the letters 'AWOL' stand for?

Since before the American civil war, this abbreviation has been used by armies to signify 'Absent Without Official Leave'. Confederate soldiers caught while AWOL were made to walk about the camp carrying a sign bearing these letters.

B

Babes in the woods
When would we call people 'babes in the wood'?
This is a name for innocent and defenceless people who cannot cope with the circumstances in which they find themselves. According to tradition, the events of the Babes in the Wood folk tale originally happened in Wayland Wood in Norfolk, England. After the death of their parents, two children were left in the care of their uncle. The uncle paid two men to take the children to the woods and kill them, but they were unable to bring themselves to go through with it and instead just abandoned the children. The children eventually died, however, as they were incapable of fending for themselves. *Hansel and Gretel*, by the Brothers Grimm, is a reworking of the story – with a far happier ending.

Bachelor
Why is the college degree called a 'bachelor's' degree?
Because originally a 'bachelor' was a soldier not old enough or rich enough to lead his retainers into battle under his own banner. Therefore, the word meant a person of inferior rank. It was applied to the college degree in order to differentiate it from the higher degree of 'doctor'.

Back of beyond
Where is the real 'back of beyond'?
The Australian Outback. The expression originated in Australia in the nineteenth century, but is commonly used now to describe any remote, under-populated and backward area.

Back to the drawing board
When was 'back to the drawing board' first used to mean 'start all over again'?
The term has been used since World War II as an acceptance, all too frequently said with a resigned sigh, that a design has failed and a new one is needed. A drawing board is the sloping architect's or draughtsman's desk that is used for the preparation of designs or blueprints.

Back number

Where did we get 'back number' as a name for a person who is behind the times?

From the newspaper and magazine trade. Because each succeeding issue of a periodical bears a consecutively greater number, old copies are referred to as 'back numbers'.

Back up

Why is a person who becomes stubborn and angry said to get his 'back up'?

The allusion is to the attitude of a cat when angry – it not only raises its hair, as do most animals, but also arches its back.

Back to the wall

When did the expression 'back to the wall' originate?

In the sixteenth century. It was used to describe someone so cornered that his only option was to stand and fight. The metaphor is used today for someone in an overwhelmingly difficult situation.

Back the wrong horse

Does 'back the wrong horse' have a racing origin?

Yes. If you had backed the wrong horse, you had made a bad decision and chosen one that didn't win. So, in more general usage, backing the wrong horse means opting for a course of action that cannot possibly succeed.

Backing and filling

Why do we say an indecisive person is 'backing and filling'?

The term refers to a method of tacking a sailing ship when the tide is with the vessel and the wind against it – in which the ship moves ahead slowly by fits and starts. The sails are allowed to 'fill' with wind and then the wind is spilled from them by hauling 'back' on the rigging.

Bad hair day

What is a 'bad hair day'?

It's a day when everything goes wrong – and sometimes the more you try to put things right the worse they get. This fairly modern expression perhaps became so popular because those days when one's hair just won't do what you want it to are so familiar to all – particularly teenage girls.

Badge of poverty

How did we come by the expression 'badge of poverty'?

At one time in England bankrupts and beggars were compelled to wear the 'dyvour' or 'badge of poverty'. This consisted of a half-yellow and half-brown coat and upper hose of the same colours.

Bags

Why do children say 'I "bags" this' – meaning 'it's mine'?

The word comes from poaching. Whatever a poacher managed to steal would be quickly slipped into his bag to conceal it – he would literally 'bag' it.

Baker's dozen
How did 13 come to be called a 'baker's dozen'?
The baker's dozen is believed to have originated in the thirteenth century, when the penalties for giving short weight on bread were heavy. Bakers would add one extra loaf to every twelve to make absolutely sure they stayed on the right side of the law.

Bald as a coot
What is the reason a very bald man is said to be as 'bald as a coot'?
It is because a coot is a waterfowl with a white bill that goes quite a way up its black forehead – making it appear bald.

Balk
Why do we say we 'balk' someone's efforts when we thwart them?
Because the word 'balk' comes from the Anglo-Saxon *balca*, meaning 'beam' – and, in the days before locks and keys, a balca or beam was put across the door of a hut to bar enemies and thieves.

Ball
How did a dancing party come to be called a 'ball'?
The Latin verb *ballare* means 'to dance' – but our ball had its origin in the Feast of Fools at Easter. As part of this celebration, choirboys danced around the Dean in church; he threw a ball at them and they sang as they caught it. At early American dances too, a ball was thrown as the dancers stepped in sets. Though they stopped throwing the ball, they kept the name 'ball' for the dance itself.

Balls to the wall
Does 'balls to the wall' refer to male anatomy?
No. The expression derives from aviation and the 'balls' here top the levers controlling the throttle and fuel mixtures. Pushing the balls forwards towards the walls of the cockpit increases the speed of the plane. The general meaning is 'pushed to the limit, at full speed'.

Bandy words
Why do we say we 'bandy words' when we argue?
Because of the game called 'bandy' in which the players, each with a crooked stick, bat a ball back and forth from side to side and try to get it past their opponents into the goal. To 'bandy' words, therefore, is to knock them back and forth as one would bandy a ball. The phrase 'keep the ball rolling' is also taken from the game of bandy.

Bankrupt
Where did we get the term 'bankrupt'?
From Italy – where moneychangers once placed the money they had available to lend on a bench called a *banca*. If one of these moneychangers was unable to continue in business, his counter was destroyed and so became a *banca rotta* – since *rotta* means 'broken'. Because of this practice, the term was applied to the moneychanger himself – he was said to be a *banca rotta*, or 'bankrupt'.

Baptism by fire
What is a 'baptism by fire'?
This phrase originates from the Greek *baptisma pyros*, in which fire was the 'grace of the Holy Spirit imparted through baptism'; later it was used of martyrdom by fire. It has been known in English since 1822, from a translation of the French *baptême du feu*. It was originally applied to a soldier's first experience under fire in battle. Now it describes a first encounter, usually ultimately successful, with a situation or job in which all the circumstances are as difficult as they could possibly be.

Barber
How did the 'barber' get his name?
At first, the 'barber' only trimmed beards and let the other hair alone – and the Latin word for 'beard' is *barba*. When beards were shaved off and hair began to be trimmed, the 'barber' altered his work somewhat but kept the same name.

Bare-faced lie
Why do we call an untruth a 'bare-faced lie'?
It is easy enough to lie when you do not have to show your face – for your face may give you away. So a 'bare-faced lie' is one that you make without any visible sign of compunction.

Bark is worse than his bite
When was 'his bark is worse than his bite' first used?
The expression has been used since ancient Roman times. It was inspired by noisy but affectionate pets, and is used to describe someone whose fuss and noise is out of all proportion to the actual threat he or she represents.

Barking up the wrong tree
What is the origin of the expression 'barking up the wrong tree'?
The allusion is to dogs trained to hunt raccoons and opossums and to leave other scents alone. They will occasionally pick up the scent of another animal and chase it to a tree in which it takes refuge. When the hunters eventually catch up with the pack they find the dogs 'barking up the wrong tree'.

Barnstormer
How did actors get the name 'barnstormers'?
Actors have long been called 'stormers' because of their ranting and storming. And in the early days of the theatre in England there were not enough playhouses to hold all the troupes of players that toured the country. Poor troupes and those going far afield often played in barns; these players were therefore 'barnstormers'.

Batman
Why is an army officer's soldier-servant called a 'batman'?
Because originally it was the soldier–servant's duty to look after the pack horses – and the French word for a packsaddle is *bât*.

Bazooka
How did the 'bazooka' get its name?
When Bob Burns, the vaudeville performer, devised a form of kazoo that had a very long sounding-horn he named it a 'bazooka' – from the Dutch word *bazu* meaning 'trumpet'. The 'kazoo' – a horn into which you sing and vibrate a strip of paper – gets its name from the same word. The rocket gun devised by the American Army during World War II was named for Burns' quasi-musical instrument because of its similarity in appearance.

Beam ends
Why do we say that a person who has been knocked flat has been knocked on his 'beam ends'?
The beams of a ship run across it, under the deck, from side to side. So, when the beams are on end the ship is turned on its side and cannot right itself. A person who has been knocked flat is in a very similar predicament.

Bear
Why is a Wall Street trader who sells stocks short called a 'bear'?
It's from an old folk saying: 'He sold the skin before he got the bear.' A Wall Street 'bear' sells stocks without actually having them – in the hope that the price will go down and he or she can purchase what is needed for delivery at a lower cost.

Beard the lion
What is the origin of the expression to 'beard the lion'?
The full saying is 'beard the lion in his den'. An ancient form of insult was to walk up to a man and tug at his beard; only the weak and cowardly would stand for it. A man who would insult a lion in this manner was indeed brave; one who would attempt it in the lion's den, doubly brave.

Beating about the bush
Why do we say a person who avoids the issue is 'beating about the bush'?
In many forms of hunting it is necessary to follow the game into the underbrush in order to find it, beating the bushes noisily to scare the animals out. A person afraid of the animals lurking there will 'beat about the bush', pretending to go in to find and kill the beast – but not actually doing so.

Beauty is only skin deep
Is 'beauty is only skin deep' a modern expression?
No. This warning against being taken in by appearances has been in use for over four hundred years.

Bedlam
Why does 'bedlam' mean 'riotous noise'?
Because Bedlam was the name of a London lunatic asylum. About the year 1247, the St Mary of Bethlehem priory was founded in London. The name was soon shortened to 'Bethlehem' – and then 'Bedlam'. Some three hundred years later, the priory was turned into a house of detention for the insane – and the loud and wild ravings of its inmates gave 'bedlam' its present meaning.

Bee in your bonnet
Why is behaving irrationally having a 'bee in your bonnet'?
If you had a bee trapped in your hat it is unlikely that you would be calm – or able to think about anything else! This cliché has been used since the eighteenth century to refer to someone who has become fixated on a particular idea or scheme.

Beer and skittles
What are the skittles in the expression 'life's not all beer and skittles'?
Skittles is a traditional English game similar to ten-pin bowling – as life does not consist entirely of feasting and playing, it's not all 'beer and skittles'.

Bee's knees
Why do we say that something perfect is the 'bee's knees'?
There is no real explanation for this slang expression. It appears to date from the frivolous language used by some young people following the dark days of World War I. The 'cat's pyjamas' and 'the cat's whiskers' mean the same thing, but no doubt the pleasing idiocy of 'bee's knees' is reinforced by the rhyme.

Before the mast
Why do we speak of a seaman as sailing 'before the mast'?
Because a man who goes to sea as a common seaman is quartered in the forward portion of the ship – literally 'before the mast'.

Belfry
Does the word 'belfry' come from the bells usually hung there?
No. 'Belfry' was originally the name of a military tower erected near the walls of a besieged city by the attackers. This was so that they could more easily throw their spears and shoot their arrows at the defenders. It may have come to be applied to church steeples because of their resemblance to these towers.

Bell, book and candle
What is the origin of the expression 'bell, book and candle'?
The expression is an allusion to a ceremony of excommunication introduced into the Catholic Church in the eighth century. After reading the sentence of excommunication a bell is rung, a book closed and a candle extinguished. From that moment the excommunicated person is excluded from the sacraments and even divine worship.

Belladonna
How did the 'belladonna' plant get this name?
The plant got this name because ladies once used the extract to enlarge the pupils of their eyes and so make them beautiful. *Belladonna* is Italian for 'beautiful lady'.

Below the belt
What do we mean when we say something is 'below the belt'?
That it is unfair or deceitful. The saying grew out of the rules of boxing devised by the Marquess of Queensberry in 1867. The rules prohibited punches below the line of the belt because of the particular vulnerability of the groin.

Bender
How did a heavy drinking spree come to be called a 'bender'?
It is because the drinker 'bends his elbow' every time he picks up his glass to take a drink.

Benefit of clergy
What is the origin of the expression 'benefit of clergy'?
The clergy was once allowed the privilege of exemption from trial by a secular court when arraigned for a felony – and so went free. This was the original 'benefit of clergy'. Later this privilege was extended to any first offender who, like the clergy, could read. The test for this ability was the first verse of the Fifty-first Psalm; and so, since the ability to read it could save a man's neck, the verse was called the 'neck verse'.

Beserk
Why is someone in a frenzy going 'beserk'?
A *beserker* was a Norse warrior famous for his ferocity in battle. His name came from the Icelandic *bear-sark* (bear-skin) coat he wore; he used no armour or other protection.

Beside himself
Why do we describe a distraught person as being 'beside himself'?
Because the ancients believed that soul and body could part and that under great emotional stress the soul would actually leave the body. When this happened a person was 'beside himself'. This same idea is expressed in 'out of his mind'; and in 'ecstasy' too. 'Ecstasy' is from the Greek, meaning 'to stand out of'.

Better place
What is the 'better place'?
It's heaven. This sentimental expression, meaning 'died and gone to heaven', originated in Shakespeare's *Measure for Measure*.

Between a rock and a hard place
Why do we say we're 'between a rock and a hard place' when all available options are bad?
The reference is to the Greek hero Odysseus having to choose whether to sail close to the monster Scylla or the whirlpool Charybdis. They are equally unattractive and dangerous, but in the event Odysseus successfully negotiates a way through them – though not without the loss of six members of his crew.

Beyond the pale
Why do we say an uncouth person or act is 'beyond the pale'?
In the twelfth century, when the English first went into Ireland, they established themselves in the region around Dublin. This was known as the 'pale'. English authority existed only 'within the pale' and the remainder of Ireland was governed by local kings and leaders of clans, some of whom were regarded as very uncouth. So 'beyond the pale' came to mean outside of the civilised zone of British jurisdiction.

Bias
How did the word 'bias' come to mean crooked?
In bowling, a weight was once placed within the ball to make it deviate from a straight line. This was called the 'bias'. Today anything that makes a person deviate from accepted thought or behaviour is called a 'bias'.

Big Brother
Why should we be worried when being watched by 'Big Brother'?
Because you are being spied on and controlled by someone more powerful than you. It comes from George Orwell's novel *1984* (published in 1949), in which the State controls every aspect of people's lives.

Big cheese
Why is the most important person in a group called the 'big cheese'?
The expression has nothing to do with dairy products. 'Cheese' is a corruption of the Persian or Hindi word *chiz*, meaning 'thing'. So a 'big cheese' is used to describe a 'big thing'. Its use today nearly always has slightly derisory undertones.

Bigwig
Why do we call an important person a 'bigwig'?
In Great Britain it was long the custom for all men of importance to wear special wigs – indeed, British judges and lawyers still wear them. So, a person of importance had a 'big wig' – and was called one.

Billingsgate
What is the origin of the term 'billingsgate' for coarse, abusive talk?
The firm of Lud & Billins built a gate in the wall around the City of London that soon came to be called 'Billingsgate'. The London fish market was established nearby and the fishmongers there were noted for their loud and vulgar language.

Bite the bullet
When people have to face an unpleasant inevitability, why do we advise them to 'bite the bullet'?
In the days before reliable anaesthetics, injured soldiers would bite on a bullet to help them endure pain. Perhaps this is still done in emergencies, but – thankfully – with improvements in battlefield medicine the true meaning of the phrase is now redundant.

Bite the dust
What do we mean by making someone 'bite the dust'?
This is an allusion by the ancient Greek poet Homer to defeating an enemy and making him sprawl face-down on the ground. In this position he would almost certainly get a mouthful of dust.

Bitter end
Where does the 'bitter' of the expression 'to the bitter end' come from?
From the timber to which the anchor rope or chain of early sailing ships was fastened. It was called the 'bitt', and when the anchor was let out as far as the line or chain could go, it was played out 'to the bitter end'.

Black Maria
What is the reason a police van is called a 'Black Maria'?
The police van is supposed to have been given this name in honour of one Marie (or Maria) Lee, a black woman of great size and strength, who ran a sailors' boarding house in Boston, USA. The unruly stood in dread of her, and when the constables required help they often sent for 'Black Maria' – who soon collared the culprits and led them to the lock-up.

Black sheep
Why is someone who is regarded as a disgrace or failure by his or her family the 'black sheep'?
Black sheep may once have been feared because black was considered the colour of the devil; black sheep were also believed to bite people. The most likely explanation for the saying is that the wool of black sheep cannot be dyed and so does not bring as high a price as regular wool. Yet a black sheep eats as much and takes as much time and care as any other; therefore, it is hardly worth its keep.

Blackball
Why do we say that a person rejected for membership of a secret society has been 'blackballed'?
Because many secret societies still follow the practice of balloting by using black and white balls dropped into the ballot box. The white stands for acceptance; the black for rejection. This custom is very old – it was used by the ancient Greeks and Romans. Even our word 'ballot' means 'a little ball'. So, too, does the word 'bullet'.

Blackguard
How did the 'blackguard' get this name?

When a noble household moved from one residence to another, the scullions and kitchen knaves travelled in the wagons with their pots and pans. Since these lowly menials were always ragged and usually extremely dirty, this portion of the train was jocularly called the 'black guards'. Thievery was common among them and they were generally unscrupulous – thus 'blackguard' came to mean a villainous person.

Blackout
How did we get the term 'blackout'?

The expression was originally used in the theatre – where it was applied to the extinguishing of all lights on stage while the scenery was being shifted. Then, in 1939, the British applied it to the precautionary measures they adopted to conceal strategic targets from bombing by enemy aircraft.

Blarney
Why are soft and sweet words called 'blarney'?

In the castle of the little village of Blarney, near Cork in Ireland, there is an inscribed stone in a position that is difficult to access – and there is a popular saying that anyone who kisses the Blarney Stone will ever after possess a cajoling tongue. There is also a legend regarding the first to ply this art. In the year 1602, Cormack Macarthy found he could no longer hold the castle of Blarney against the British. He was forced to negotiate an armistice by which he agreed to surrender the fort to them. But, though the British emissary, Carew, received from Macarthy many soft words and sweet promises, he never got the castle.

Blessing in disguise
What is a 'blessing in disguise'?

This expression has been in use since the eighteenth century. Its meaning is very similar to 'every cloud has a silver lining' – that something you think is going to be bad turns out unexpectedly well after all.

Blimp
How did the non-rigid balloon come to be called the 'blimp'?

When England began experimenting with this type of airship in 1914, two designs were tested – the 'A-limp' and the 'B-limp'. The 'A-limp' was unsuccessful but the 'B-limp' was used and gave its name to all airships of this type.

Blind alley
Why is an alley closed off at one end called a 'blind alley'?

A gate or opening in a wall was at one time called an 'eye'. If there was no opening in the wall at the end of an alley – and so no 'eye' – it was, of course, 'blind'.

Blind justice
How did justice come to be called 'blind'?
Justice is usually represented in Greek statues as wearing a blindfold and holding a pair of scales. Justice was blindfolded so she couldn't see the bribes that were being offered to her. The ancient Egyptians carried this idea even further; they conducted their trials in a darkened chamber so that the witnesses, the pleader and the prisoner could not be seen by the judges. The Egyptians felt that this would result in an impartial decision, with no misplaced sympathy – though the system must also have resulted in an occasional misplaced prisoner.

Blizzard
Who invented the word 'blizzard'?
O.C. Bates, editor of the *Northern Vindicator* of Estherville, Iowa, USA. Bates coined, or at least popularised, the word 'blizzard' in describing the snowstorm in Estherville on 14 March 1870. He may have had in mind the German word *blitz*, meaning 'lightning' – or, from a similar root, the English dialect prefix *bliz*, meaning something 'violent in action'.

Bloomers
How did 'bloomers' get their name?
Mrs Elizabeth Miller Smith really invented the 'bloomers', but Mrs Amelia Jenks Bloomer did so much to popularise them – by both wearing them and writing about them – that her name was given to these garments.

Blow by blow
What is a 'blow by blow' account?
It's a very detailed description of an event. The term originated in radio boxing commentary; in the absence of visuals, the commentator had to precisely describe every single move by each of the fighters.

Blow hot and cold
Why is a person who changes his mind said to 'blow hot and cold'?
When you blow with your lips pursed, your breath seems cold. When you do not blow as definitely, but leave the mouth loose, you blow hot. So, when a person starts to say something and then stops, his mouth first puckers and then becomes flaccid – and he 'blows hot and cold'.

Blue blood
Why is a member of the aristocracy called a 'blue blood'?
Because the Spanish once had the idea that the veins of men and women from aristocratic families were bluer than those of other people.

Blue Book
What is the reason an official report of the British Government is called a 'Blue Book'?
It is because reports of the British Parliament and Privy Council are issued bound with a dark blue paper cover. A preliminary or less extensive report is issued without a cover and is called a White Paper.

Blue chip

Why is a reliable financial venture 'blue chip'?

It's a gambling expression. In counter games such as poker the blue chip is the most valuable. A 'blue chip' venture is almost certain to succeed and be extremely profitable.

Blue Peter

How did hoisting the 'Blue Peter' come to mean getting ready to go?

The expression is a seafaring one. A ship about to leave port hoists a blue flag with a white square in the centre – the code for the letter 'P' – which is correctly called the 'blue repeater'. This stands for the French word *partir*, meaning 'to depart'. The flag was originally hoisted by a ship to recall seamen who had gone ashore. It also gives notice to the town that all with claims for money against the ship should come and make them before it departed.

Blue ribbon

Why is something special called a 'blue ribbon' this or that – as a 'blue ribbon' jury?

Because an Englishman who was made a Knight of the Garter was given a blue rosette to wear at the knee. Also because Knights of the Grand Cross, the French Order of the Holy Ghost, at one time the highest order in France, wore a blue ribbon as a badge of membership.

Blues

Why do we call despondency the 'blues'?

Because 'blue devils' were once a common form of apparition experienced by those suffering from *delirium tremens* or 'the morning after' – though of late these imps have become 'pink elephants'!

Bluestocking

How did we get the name 'bluestocking' for a female academic?

Indirectly from Venice. Back in 1400 there was a society of ladies and gentlemen in Venice called *Della Calza*, distinguished by the blue stockings its members wore. In 1590, the custom was introduced into Paris, where women of learning adopted it. Then, in 1750, a group of English women picked up the idea and formed what they called the *Bas-bleu* Club. They too, as well as the men of their circle, wore blue stockings. This created quite a scandal – since blue was originally the colour of servants and others of low circumstances. The women who belonged to this group all made a point of making their conversations serious – and so today a female academic is called a 'bluestocking'.

Blurb

What is the origin of the word 'blurb'?

When Gellette Burgess's *Are You A Bromide?* was published, he devised a special dust jacket for some 500 presentation copies to be given away at a booksellers' banquet. Since it was then the custom to have a picture of a woman on the jacket of every novel, Burgess featured a sickly-sweet portrait of a young woman and in the accompanying text described her as 'Miss Belinda Blurb'. From this the usual dust jacket 'blow up' of an author and his book came to be called a 'blurb'.

Bobby

Why are London policeman called 'bobbies'?

Because the London police force was organised by Sir Robert Peel. The 'bobby' was taken from his first name. There is also another, even older, term for London policemen that is no longer used but was at one time quite popular – 'peelers' from Sir Robert's last name.

Bob's your uncle

What is the origin of 'Bob's your uncle'?

The origin is uncertain, but this catchphrase is certainly several hundred years old and is still in current use. One possible derivation is the appointment by the Victorian prime minister Lord Salisbury (Robert Cecil) of his nephew Arthur Balfour to a series of high-profile government posts. It was considered that Balfour was unsuitable for these positions, which he would not have been offered had 'Bob' not been his 'uncle'. The phrase is used today almost as an exclamation of how simple something is: 'You just do this and Bob's your uncle!'

Body and soul

What is the origin of the expression 'keep body and soul together'?

It was once believed that the soul could easily slip out of the body – and the devil could then move in. This was very undesirable and so it was essential for everyone to 'keep body and soul together'. That's why we say 'God bless you' when a person sneezes. The ancients believed that with a sneeze the soul was forced out of the body through the nostrils, and the devil – who was lurking around every corner – would take this opportunity to slip in and block the return of the soul. If, however, a friend blessed you when you sneezed, then – because of your momentary holiness – the devil could not enter and your soul could return to your body once again.

Bombast

Why is a ranting speech said to be full of 'bombast'?

Because the soft down of the cotton plant is called 'bombast' and this was much used in the sixteenth century for padding clothes. From this, padded speeches came to be called 'bombast'.

Bone to pick

Why does a person wishing to reprimand you say 'I have a bone to pick with you'?

Two people picking over a single bone will bend their heads over, closer and closer together. Two people who are engrossed in serious conversation will do the same. In addition, if two people are disputing a point they may 'growl' at each other like two dogs fighting over a bone.

Bone up

Where did students get the expression 'bone up', meaning to study for examinations?

From the publishing firm named Bohn, which first published the 'trots' (revision guides) that helped students pass their Greek and Latin courses. Though the students called it 'Bohn up' at first, the term was soon changed to 'bone up' because of the obvious pun on 'bonehead'.

Boogie-woogie

What is the origin of the term 'boogie-woogie'?

A 'boogie' is a bogie, a hobgoblin, anything magic. Witches, goblins and other 'boogies' dance to weird, disquieting music. So, music with something of the beat of the tom-toms in the bass is 'boogie' music. 'Woogie' is just a ricochet of 'boogie'.

Boondoggle

Where did the word 'boondoggle' originate?

Among Boy Scouts. The braided leather lanyard worn by Boy Scouts has no real purpose. It was named a 'boondoggle' by Robert H. Link of Rochester – possibly after Daniel Boone and 'joggle'. During the depression of the 1930s, the name of this useless piece of equipment was transferred to the innumerable useless tasks performed by men employed on 'make-work' projects of the American Federal Government.

Bootlegger

Why is a dealer in illicit alcohol called a 'bootlegger'?

It was and still is against the law to sell liquor to Native American Indians – especially on their reservations. However, in the days when men wore high boots it was easy to smuggle in a flat pint or quart bottle by slipping it into the leg of the boot.

Born to the purple

What is the origin of the expression 'born to the purple'?

The phrase does not refer to the purple robes worn by royalty – but to a special lying-in room designed by a Byzantine empress. The room was lined with porphyry – a purple stone – and this was the first colour the children of the empress cast their eyes upon after birth.

Boss
How did the 'boss' get his name?
From the fact that at one time he had complete authority over his workers and could thrash them at will. 'Boss' comes from the old High German *bozan*, which means 'to beat'.

Boudoir
Why is a 'boudoir' so called?
The term comes from the French *bouder*, meaning to pout or sulk, so it is a room to which a lady may retire when feeling petulant. The first boudoirs were those of the mistresses of Louis XV of France.

Bowdlerise
What is the origin of the term 'bowdlerise'?
Doctor Thomas Bowdler edited an edition of Shakespeare, removing from it 'those expressions which cannot with propriety be read aloud in the family'. From this we get the term 'bowdlerise', meaning 'to emasculate by over-editing'.

Bowled over
Where did the expression 'bowled over' come from?
It originated in cricket. We use it to describe complete surprise about something or someone. Although being bowled over is the last thing a batsman wants, when we apply it to other situations we can mean it in a positive way – bowled over by love, for instance.

Boycott
How did the word 'boycott' get its meaning?
The name – and its meaning – came from the first victim of the practice. In 1880 Lord Erne, an absentee Irish landlord, employed as his agent at Lough Mask in Connemara a certain Captain Boycott. Boycott asked such unreasonable rentals from the tenants that they refused to pay anything at all. The Irish Land League adopted the practice of refusal and began using the phrase 'let's Boycott him' – meaning 'let's do it to him as we did to Captain Boycott'.

Brand new
Why do we say 'brand new' to mean very new?
Formerly the use of 'brand new' was limited to things made of metal. 'Brand' is an old Anglo-Saxon word that means 'burn'. So a horseshoe, ploughshare or sword just forged was said to be 'brand new' – that is, fresh from the fire. The term was later applied to all new things.

Brass hat
Why is an army officer called a 'brass hat'?
Most high-ranking army officers have large amounts of gilt ornamentation on their caps. Since the common soldier always disparages those above him, he calls this ornamentation 'brass' – and the officer a 'brass hat'.

Brass tacks

Where did we get the expression 'getting down to brass tacks'?

From early English drapers' shops. The linen draper placed brass tacks along the inner edge of his counter and used them to measure off the fabric his customers wished to buy. When a customer had finished looking over his stock and was ready to state the amount of cloth he or she wished to buy this was 'getting down to brass tacks'.

Breadline

Why do we say we are on the 'breadline' when we have no money?

'Line' is the American equivalent for queue. A breadline was a queue of poor people waiting for free food to be handed out.

Break a leg

Why do actors say 'break a leg' instead of wishing each other good luck?

One theory is that actors, members of a notoriously superstitious profession, believe that saying 'good luck' will bring bad luck. Instead they wish a piece of 'bad' luck, which breaking a leg would certainly be, in the hope that the fates will reverse the request. Another theory is that an actor who has performed well will be expected to bow over and over again to the appreciative audience – and in the process of a full, elaborate bow one leg is placed behind the other and both knees are bent.

Breaking the ice

How did making the way easy for a person come to be called 'breaking the ice'?

Whaling ships and others sailing to Arctic regions often find ice clogging the channel through which they wish to pass – and so must send boats ahead to break the ice for them.

Bridge of Sighs

What is the origin of the term 'Bridge of Sighs'?

In Venice, a bridge connects the Palace of the Doges with the state prison and condemned prisoners on their way to execution once passed over this bridge. In the centre of the bridge there is a single window and prisoners frequently paused at this window to 'sigh' as they caught their last glimpse of the world.

Bring home the bacon

Where did we get the expression 'bring home the bacon'?

From country fairs. It was once the practice at fairs to grease a pig and let it loose among a number of blindfolded contestants. The man who successfully caught the greased pig could keep it – and so, of course, 'bring home the bacon'.

Bring the house down
Why is thunderous applause said to 'bring the house down'?

It is a bit of an exaggeration. If the applause of the audience is thunderous enough and the people stamp their feet as well as clap their hands and whistle, their actions may threaten to topple a rickety theatre and literally 'bring the house down'.

Brown study
How did we come to call a gloomy reverie a 'brown study'?

The term is a translation of the French term *sombre reverie*. *Sombre* not only means 'dull in colour' but also 'sad' and 'gloomy'. And so 'brown study' means gloomy or intense thought.

Brownie points
Did the expression 'brownie points' originate with the Girl Scout movement?

Yes. Girl Scouts perform tasks to accumulate points that advance them in the organisation. The phrase entered general language from World War II slang, because so many of the regulations and tasks appeared to the enlisted men to be childlike and emasculating. Nowadays, we might perform chores that we don't particularly want to do or see the value in, in the hope that they will accumulate the credit to allow us to do something we really do want.

Buck the system
Does 'buck the system' have anything to do with horse riding?

Yes. When we 'buck the system' we refuse to comply with regulations, in the same way that a bucking horse will try to unseat its rider instead of calmly doing as it should.

Bucket shop
Why is a 'bucket shop' called that?

In underworld slang, to 'bucket' is to cheat. A firm professing to be a brokerage office, but not a member of an Exchange, cannot actually place its customers' orders to buy and sell. The customers are therefore merely betting on a rise or fall in prices – and are cheated out of owning anything tangible.

Budget
How did we get the word 'budget'?

It has long been the custom for the British Chancellor of the Exchequer to bring his papers regarding financial expenditures to the House of Commons in a leather bag or portfolio, which he places on the table before him. The 'budget' was named for this leather bag – for the old French word for a 'bag' is *bougette*. To 'open the budget' is a literal description of the procedure the Chancellor follows – he opens the bag and takes out his papers.

Bulldoze
What is the origin of the term 'bulldoze'?
The term was originally 'bulldose' – and it meant a 'dose' of whipping sufficient for a bull. It was applied in America to the whippings the vigilantes gave black people who were seeking office during the reconstruction period after the Civil War. The term was later applied to persons using duress – and from this idea of pushing others around 'bulldoze' became associated with the machine.

Bull's eye
Why is the centre spot of a target called the 'bull's eye'?
Aboard sailing ships, a 'bull's eye' is an oval wooden block with a groove around it and a hole in the centre through which a small line may be drawn. A target with a centre spot looks something like this block and the block looks something like an actual bull's eye – hence the name.

Bumph
Why do we call endless paperwork 'bumph'?
It's a term that originated in the armed services to describe printed matter considered surplus to requirement – which might as well be used as toilet paper. From 'bum-fodder' it became 'bumph'.

Burn bridges
What do we do when we 'burn bridges'?
We take actions that permanently cut off a relationship. The expression is less than 150 years old, though it refers to the Roman military practice of burning a bridge once it had been crossed out of enemy territory, thus making it impossible for the enemy army to follow.

Bury the hatchet
Why do we 'bury the hatchet' when we end a quarrel?
The saying derives from the Native American Indian custom of burying a tomahawk to symbolise the binding nature of a peace treaty.

Bushwhacker
Why is the person who lives in wild country called a 'bushwhacker'?
Because almost every person who goes to open up new territory has to chop or 'whack' out the bushes to make their way and create a clearing for their home.

Busman's holiday
What is a 'busman's holiday'?
It is when someone chooses to spend their leisure time doing what they do in their line of work. It is believed to have originated in the days of horse-drawn buses, when drivers who had become fond of their horses would spend their days off travelling as passengers on their own buses, so as not to be separated from the animals.

Butcher's dog

We say 'as fit as a butcher's dog' but why should this animal be considered the epitome of health?

The dog is likely to receive copious meat scraps from its butcher owner, so it should be well fed (rather than merely overweight). Another connected reference – 'like a butcher's dog' – means that the unfortunate animal is in close contact with the meat but is not allowed to touch it. It is used to illustrate being temptingly close to something desirable but forbidden.

Butter wouldn't melt in his mouth

We say this of prim and proper people. Why?

This phrase goes back to at least the mid-sixteenth century, when it was usually appied to a woman – though these days we would be just as likely to apply it to a man. It implies that the person is so lacking in warmth that they couldn't even melt butter.

By and large

What does the expression 'by and large' mean?

This derives from sailing ship days when, depending on the way the vessel faced on to a particular wind direction, it was sailing either 'by the wind' or 'large' – but it could never do both at the same time. The phrase in sailors' jargon meant 'in all possible circumstances', which the layman adopted to convey the idea of 'on the whole' or 'all things considered'.

Cack-handed

Why is a clumsy person 'cack-handed'?

Cack is an Old English word for dung, taken from the Latin *cacare*, meaning 'to defecate'. In some cultures it is the custom to use the left hand for cleaning after defecation, the right hand being reserved for eating. To be left-handed was therefore to be 'cack-handed', which was extended to mean awkward or inept.

Calendar

How did the 'calendar' get its name?

From the Latin word for an interest book kept by moneylenders – the *calendarium*. Interest fell due on the *calends* or first day of the month. *Calends* itself came from *calare* – the Latin verb meaning 'to call' – because the Romans used to publicly 'call out' the first day of the month.

Call it a day

What do we mean by let's 'call it a day'?

The speaker is suggesting that this would be a good point to stop a task for the time being, though it may not be completely finished. It was probably first used by people employed by the day, who might reach a sensible cut-off point in a job before the end of the working day.

Call a spade a spade

Is it politically correct to use the phrase 'call a spade a spade'?

Etymologically speaking, yes it is. The phrase originates from the times of the ancient Greeks and therefore has no racist connotations whatsoever; however, so many people think it has that it should still be used cautiously to avoid offence. Ironically, it means speaking plainly and without euphemism. It has been used by as diverse people as Plutarch and Oscar Wilde.

Canopy

Why is a bed curtain called a 'canopy'?

The word comes to us from the Greeks and literally means a 'gnat-curtain'. The fishermen of the Nile used to sleep under a makeshift tent made out of their fishnets, believing – perhaps without too much foundation – that gnats would not be able to pass through the holes.

Canter
Where did we get the word 'canter', meaning a loping trot?
It is a shortening of 'Canterbury'. The pilgrims on their way to the tomb of Thomas à Becket in Canterbury rode at this speed – and so gave their name to the gait.

Carat
What is the origin of the word 'carat'?
The 'carat' was originally a measure of value and not weight. A symbol used to represent a unit of money in the time of the Roman emperor Constantine looked like a picture of the fruit of the locust tree. The Arabic name for this fruit is *qirat* – whence 'carat'.

Carbon footprint
What do we mean by our 'carbon footprint'?
It is a measure of the environmental damage created by a person simply through his or her life style. The calculation takes into consideration such factors as travel and other forms of fuel consumption, food miles (how much food you buy from non-local sources) and diet. Scientifically speaking, it is the amount of carbon dioxide produced by the combustion of fossil fuels by an individual or organisation.

Carte blanche
How did we come to use the phrase 'carte blanche' to mean complete freedom of choice?
It has long been the custom for a man of importance to give a trusted subordinate blank sheets of paper or correspondence cards with his name signed at the bottom – thus giving the subordinate the right to fill in whatever he wished above the signature. Since there is no writing on the paper or card, it is a 'white paper' or 'white card' – in French, *carte blanche*.

Cash cow
What does the financial term 'cash cow' mean?
In business, a cash cow is a product or service that, despite needing little maintenance, generates good profits. The allusion is to a dairy cow, which is acquired with an initial capital outlay, but then produces milk over its lifetime with little further investment in time or money.

Catch-22
Who coined the phrase 'catch-22'?
Joseph Heller in his novel of the same name, to describe a deadlock regulation that makes one a victim whatever choice he makes. Heller's model catch-22 specified that concern for one's safety showed a rational mind. An insane pilot would qualify for grounding, but to obtain the necessary certificate of insanity he had to request it from the squadron doctor on these grounds. However, if he was rational enough to make the request then he was clearly sane – and must continue flying.

Catch word
How did a 'catch word' come to be called that?
The term comes to us from the theatre. The last word of an actor's speech in the theatre is the cue word that indicates another player's turn to speak. The player must 'catch' this word in order to know when it is his turn. But actors themselves probably took the term from printing – for it was once customary to print at the bottom of a page the first word of the first line of the next page.

Catgut
What have cats got to do with 'catgut'?
Not a thing; orchestral stringed instruments use sheep gut. But one name for a stringed instrument is 'kit' – from the Latin name for a guitar, *cithara*. The gut strings of the instrument are therefore 'kit guts'. A simple wrong deduction led to 'catgut'.

Cat's cradle
How did the children's game come to be called 'cat's cradle'?
The term was originally 'cratch-cradle' and 'cratch' is from the Middle English *crecche*, meaning a rack in which hay is put for cattle. The first figure created with the string in 'cat's cradle' looks like a 'cratch'.

Cat's-paw
Why is a dupe called a 'cat's-paw'?
The reference is to the ancient fable of the monkey who wanted to get some roasted chestnuts from the fire. To keep from being burned it used the paw of a cat to pull them out. 'Pulling one's chestnuts from the fire' refers to the same fable.

Caught red-handed
What do we mean by 'caught red-handed'?
That we have been detected in the very act of wrongdoing and guilt is therefore indisputable. The original reference is to being detected having committed a murder, before you have time to wash away the victim's blood.

Caviare to the general
Is the 'general' in this saying a high-ranking military officer?
No. It's a contraction of 'general public'. The source is *Hamlet*: 'The play, I remember, pleased not the million; 'twas caviare to the general.' And the meaning is that there's no point in giving a superior product to those who may not have acquired the taste for it.

Chalk and cheese
Why do we say things or people that have nothing in common are like 'chalk and cheese'?
It's a traditional phrase, no doubt popular partly because of the alliteration. It would be hard to confuse dry, jagged chalk with smooth, moist cheese when in the mouth.

Chance your arm
Was someone who 'chanced his arm' in danger of losing a limb?
No. The 'arm' in this case refers to a stripe of military rank worn on the upper sleeve. The expression means to take a risk and in the forces taking a risk by breaking a regulation could lead to punishment, demotion and ultimately loss of a stripe.

Chatterbox
What is the origin of the term 'chatterbox'?
'Chatter' is, of course, an onomatopoeic word – it sounds like what it means. The 'box' was added because of the similarly of the sound between someone chattering and the clattering of the box used by beggars in the street for collecting alms.

Chattering classes
Who coined the phrase the 'chattering classes'?
Margaret Thatcher in the 1980s, at the start of her period as British prime minister. It was a disparaging description of the liberal middle classes who raged vociferously yet impotently against many of her policies around their dinner tables.

Chauvinism
Why do we call exaggerated patriotism 'chauvinism'?
Because of Nicolas Chauvin, the first 'chauvinist'. Chauvin was a veteran of the Napoleonic wars, whose patriotism and attachment to Napoleon were so extreme that he eventually became ridiculous, even to his companions-in-arms.

Cheat
Where did we get the word 'cheat'?
From English feudal law. According to this law, if a tenant died without competent heirs or was convicted of a felony, his lands reverted to the lord. The term for such reversion was 'escheat'. To the tenant and his family this did not seem fair – and so the term 'escheat' or 'cheat' came to mean 'dishonest practices'. The word 'escheat' itself comes from the Latin *excadere*, meaning 'to fall to the lot of'.

Checkmate
Why is the winning move in chess called 'checkmate'?
'Checkmate' is used to describe the situation when one player in a game of chess has so manoeuvred his pieces, that his opponent's king cannot move without being taken from the board. The term comes from the Arabic *shah-mät*, meaning 'the king is dead'.

Cheek
What is the reason 'cheek' means impudence – as in the phrase 'none of your cheek'?
'Cheek' here is substituted for 'jaw' – and your jaw is used in talking. If you stop talking you can't be impudent.

Chemistry
Is there any scientific proof of 'chemistry' between people?
Yes. The fact that people react to each other in different biochemical ways has been confirmed by modern science, but the expression has been in use since the sixteenth century.

Cheshire cat
Where did we get the expression 'grin like a Cheshire cat'?
From the Cheshire cheeses that were moulded to look like cats with very broad grins. The cheese was cut from the tail end, so that the last part eaten was the head – or the grin.

Chestnut
How did a stale joke come to be called a 'chestnut'?
In *The Broken Sword*, a play by William Dillon, a character is forever telling the same joke about himself in connection with a cork tree. Another character says, 'A chestnut tree'. He insists it is a cork tree. The other replies: 'Chestnut – I've heard you tell the joke twenty-seven times and I'm sure it was a chestnut.'

Chewing the fat
Why, when people are gathered for a gossip, do we say that they are 'chewing the fat'?
From the early twentieth century this has meant talking informally, perhaps at length, on this, that and the other; previously it suggested grumbling or grousing. The 'fat' was probably tough dried meat such as salt pork. A variation is 'chewing the rag', the rag being the tongue.

Chicken
How did 'chicken' come to mean cowardly?
The reference is to baby chicks. They are very timid and run to hide under their mother's wing on the slightest provocation.

Chip off the old block
Does 'chip off the old block' have anything do to with carpentry?
Yes, the chip is from a block of wood. The saying is applied to someone who closely shares physical or character features with a parent or other blood relative.

Chip on his shoulder
Why do we say an easily offended person has a 'chip on his shoulder'?
At one time a youth spoiling for a fight would place a chip of wood on his shoulder and try to provoke his intended opponent to knock it off – which if done would be the signal for all hell to break loose. The signal resembles that of the medieval knight throwing down his gauntlet; if the opponent picked it up the challenge was accepted and the contest had to take place.

Chocolate teapot

Why do we say something ineffectual is 'as much use as a chocolate teapot'?

Because on contact with hot tea, the chocolate would melt! Variations on this expression are 'as much use as a chocolate fireguard' and 'as much use as an ashtray on a motorbike'.

Chowder

Where does the word 'chowder' come from?

Chowder is supposed to have been invented by the housewives of Brittany. The term comes from the French word for the cauldron in which they made their chowders, *chaudière* – which in turn comes from *chaud*, meaning 'hot'.

Church mouse

How did a 'church mouse' come to be the symbol of poverty – as in the expression, 'poor as a church mouse'?

There is no food cupboard or larder in a church vestry, so no crumbs for a mouse to feed on.

Clapped out

Why do we say we're 'clapped out' when exhausted?

When pursued in a hunt or by predators, hares often have to stop to catch their breath. While sitting upright on their haunches to keep aware of the danger, their chests heave in and out and their front legs move in time with their breaths. They appear to be clapping.

Claptrap

What is the reason we call cheap but showy words 'claptrap'?

This term originally meant a ruse or 'trap' used by actors to induce applause or 'clapping'. It was a showy piece of business or dialogue that was nevertheless intrinsically worthless.

Clearing the decks

Why do we describe preparation for action as 'clearing the decks'?

It is a nautical term. Before a naval vessel goes into action, the crew members tie down or remove all movable articles on the decks, so that they won't roll about and injure the sailors during the battle.

Clerk

How did an office assistant get the name 'clerk'?

At one time only the clergy knew how to read or write – and so any person with this ability was assumed to be a 'cleric'. From this the words 'clerical' and 'cleric' – soon shortened to 'clerk' – came to mean written work or one who performed such work.

Click

Why do we say a successful endeavour 'clicks'?

Because it runs smoothly from the start. When the gears of a machine mesh immediately, they go together with a single 'click' instead of grinding and grating.

Clodhopper

Where did someone slow-witted get the name 'clodhopper'?

In early England the peasants were uneducated; it was therefore assumed they were unintelligent. The gentry rode horses across the fields, while the peasantry walked, hopping over the clods of earth turned up by the plough. They were literally 'clodhoppers'.

Close shave

Does 'close shave' have anything to do with wood shavings?

No. The expression derives from the vulnerable position of a man who is being shaved around the throat by a barber with a cut-throat razor. It describes the narrow avoidance of danger.

Cloud cuckoo land

Who first referred to having unrealistic expectations as living on 'cloud cuckoo land'?

It was Arisophanes in his play *The Birds*. The characters Peisetairus and Euelpides, which can be translated as Mr Trusting and Mr Hopeful, are tired of living on Earth but neither do they want to dwell on Mount Olympus with the gods. They plan to build a perfect city in the clouds, between Heaven and Earth, and call it Cloud Cuckoo Land.

Clue

How did the word 'clue' come to mean a hint?

It comes from 'clew' – a ball of thread. In Greek myth, Theseus unrolled a ball of thread as he went into the Minotaur's labyrinth so he could find his way out again.

Coals to Newcastle

What is the reason a senseless task is compared to carrying 'coals to Newcastle'?

It is because Newcastle is in the centre of the great coalfields of England – and so it is as silly to carry coals there as to carry water to a well.

Cock-and-bull story

How did a fanciful tale get the name 'cock-and-bull story'?

The expression is a derisive allusion to the fables of Aesop and others in which cocks moralise and bulls debate.

Cockles of the heart

Why do we speak of warming the 'cockles of the heart'?

'Cockle' in this context is used as another name for 'heart' – from the fact that the cockleshell and the heart are similarly shaped. Indeed, the zoological name for the 'cockle' is *cardium* from *kardia*, the Greek word for 'heart'.

Cocktail

How did the 'cocktail' get its name?

The father of the 'cocktail' in the United States was Antoine Amédée Peychaud, an apothecary who came to New Orleans from the West Indies in 1795 and who was the inventor of 'Peychaud's bitters'. The term 'cocktail' itself is probably from the French *coquetel*, the name of a mixed drink long popular in the vicinity of Bordeaux. But 'cocktail' may also have come from the common practice among owners of gamecocks of feeding them a special mash containing many ingredients – including beer or ale. This mixture was called 'cock-ale'.

C.O.D.

Why is payment on delivery termed 'C.O.D.'?

In 1841, one Erastus Elmer Barclay of New York City asked William Hamden, the original express man, to deliver a package to Joseph Young in Fulton, New York. 'But,' Barclay said, 'don't let him have it until he pays $16.50. If he can't, or won't, do that, return the package to me. I want "cash on delivery".' It was another twenty years, however, before the abbreviation began to be used.

Cold blood

What is the reason a premeditated deed is said to have been done in 'cold blood'?

It was once believed that the temperature of the blood varied. When the blood became hot, a person became emotional – whence 'hot-headed'. When the blood was cold, reason held sway.

Cold enough to freeze the balls off a brass monkey

Are we being rather rude when we use this expression to describe the weather?

No! The expression derives from the time when the British Navy used cannon balls in its fighting ships. They were stored on deck beside the actual cannon and were welded to a stable upright called a brass monkey. In bitter cold the weld could snap and the balls would roll around with the movement of the ship.

Cold feet

How did a timid person come to be said to have 'cold feet'?

It is because cases of frozen feet were frequent among soldiers until the end of the nineteenth century. A man who has cold or frozen feet can't rush into battle. He proceeds slowly – or perhaps not at all.

Cold shoulder

What is the origin of the phrase 'giving the cold shoulder' to express lack of interest?

A common wayfarer stopping at a farmhouse and asking for a meal would probably be given cold food. Since a widespread food of early England was shoulder of mutton, he would be 'given a cold shoulder'.

Cold turkey

Why is abrupt withdrawal from drugs called going 'cold turkey'?

When coming off drugs, particularly heroin, without the benefit of a phased medical programme, an addict's blood is directed to the internal organs. This leaves the skin cold, white and covered in goosebumps, thus resembling the skin of a plucked turkey.

Comedy

What is the origin of the word 'comedy'?

This word is Greek and literally means 'a village singer'. Greek villages once held revels at which the village bards sang songs that told a story. Out of this practice grew Greek drama and comedy.

Cop

How did a policeman come to be called a 'cop'?

The verb 'cop' means 'to nab' – and a major function of the police has always been to 'nab' miscreants. Therefore, a policeman was called a 'copper' – soon shortened to 'cop'. There is little doubt that this nickname was strengthened by the copper badges worn by the police at a later date.

Corduroy

What is the origin of the word 'corduroy'?

This is an English word that was either originally intended or soon afterwards assumed to represent a French phrase – *corde du roi*, meaning a 'corded fabric of the king'. But there is no such French phrase.

Corny

Where did we get the slang word 'corny'?

From the ancient Sanskrit *jirna*, which means 'old and worn out'.

Credibility gap

What is a 'credibility gap'?

It's the disparity between what is stated to be the truth and the reality of the situation. Someone who repeatedly misinforms others of the true state of affairs, will eventually lose the confidence of those he wished to convince and will have created a 'credibility gap'.

Crestfallen

Why do we say a disappointed person is 'crestfallen'?

The allusion is to cockfighting. A fighting cock that has won struts about with his crest red, rigid and upright. The one that has lost scurries away with his crest drooping and wilted.

Crocodile tears
How did false sorrow get the name 'crocodile tears'?
The expression comes from what was once believed to be a fanciful tale of ancient travellers, who said that the crocodile weeps over those it eats – though it isn't sorry at all. But a crocodile does cry as it eats, for when its mouth is full the food presses at the top of the mouth and this releases tears from the lachrymal glands.

Crossing the Rubicon
Why does the expression 'crossing the Rubicon' mean no turning back?
Because when Caesar crossed the Rubicon river in 49 BC with his army – going from his own province of Gaul into Italy contrary to the prohibition of the civil government in Rome – he was, in effect, declaring war and there was no turning back.

Crummy
What is the reason we use the word 'crummy' to mean poor quality?
The term originally meant 'very fine'. It referred to the fat and fleshy part of the bread – the part that makes crumbs – as opposed to the crust. Through sarcastic use the term has acquired the opposite meaning.

Cry all the way to the bank
Why do we 'cry all the way to the bank' when indifferent to criticism?
The flamboyant and extremely wealthy American pianist Liberace coined this phrase in a telegram he sent to a critic who had soundly slated one of his concerts: 'What you said hurt me very much. I cried all the way to the bank.'

Cubit
Where did the word 'cubit' – the unit of measurement so often mentioned in the Bible – come from?
It's derived from *cubitus*, the Latin word for 'a bend'. At one time people used the arm as a measuring rod, and the distance between the elbow and the tip of the second finger was called a 'cubit'. Under the circumstances, the 'cubit' varied accordingly to the age and size of the individual doing the measuring and ranged from 18 to 22 inches.

Cuff
When do we speak 'off the cuff' and buy 'on the cuff'?
'Off the cuff' dates from the days when the cuffs of men's formal shirts were made of celluloid and were often used as notepads by their wearers. Saying something improvised, without lengthy preparation, therefore, is speaking 'off the cuff'. It was once the custom of waiters in public houses to keep a record of what was ordered on the cuffs of their shirts. For this reason, a diner who wished to have his meal charged would jokingly suggest that the amount due be put 'on the cuff' also.

Curate's egg
Why is something that is a mixture of good and bad called a 'curate's egg'?
In 1895 the British magazine *Punch* featured a George du Maurier cartoon called True Humility. It showed a young curate having breakfast in his bishop's home. The bishop says: 'I'm afraid you have a bad egg, Mr Jones.' The timid curate, desperate not to give offence, replies: 'Oh, no, my Lord, I assure you that parts of it are excellent!' The cartoon was widely appreciated because of the ridiculous notion that an egg can be anything other than either completely good or completely 'off'. This meaning has now been lost and nowadays calling something a 'curate's egg' means that it has both good and bad qualities.

Curfew
Where does the word 'curfew' come from?
From the French term *couvre feu*, meaning 'cover the fire'. In other words, 'put out the light and go to bed'.

Curiosity killed the cat
What is the origin of the expression 'curiosity killed the cat'?
It's a corruption of 'care killed the cat' – which in turn comes from the old saying that though a cat has nine lives, 'care will wear them out'. The change came about because a spiteful or backbiting woman is called a 'cat' and the belief that women are notoriously curious. Therefore, more in hope than belief, 'curiosity will kill the cat'.

Curry favour
Why do we say a man is trying to 'curry favour'?
There is a pun intended. The Middle English word *favel* means horse. 'Curry' is a horse-riding term for brushing or grooming. A groom wishing to impress his master will 'curry' his horse diligently.

Cut the mustard
Cutting mustard isn't difficult, so why say it when something comes up to expectations?
It may have its roots in the cowboy expression – 'the proper mustard', meaning the genuine thing. Or it might be a distortion of the military phrase 'to pass muster'. Or 'mustard' may refer to the plant itself, which is tough and grows close to the ground, making it difficult to harvest.

Cuts both ways
Why do we say something with more than one impact 'cuts both ways'?
The reference is to a double-edged sword. In a battle situation a single thrust with double-edged sword is likely to have far more impact than one from a sword with a single blade.

Cutting edge

What does it mean if something is on the 'cutting edge'?

That it's in the forefront of an issue, at the most advanced and up-to-date position. The cutting edge of a knife is the business edge and the image is that it cuts through the old into the new. The expression has been in use since the mid-twentieth century and from it has developed 'bleeding edge', which is used to describe something so very new and untested that it may be risky in some way.

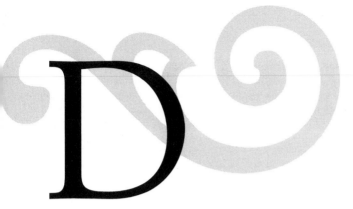

D-Day
What is the origin of the term 'D-Day'?
The 'D' in 'D-Day' just stands for 'day' – any given day – though it is now generally used to refer to the day Allied troops invaded France in World War II – 6 June 1944. In order not to divulge the designated day of a military operation it was never written as a definite date but only as 'D'; the hours designated as 'H'. Other related days and hours were designated as 'D +' or 'D -' and 'H +' or 'H -'.

Daggers drawn
What does it mean when people are 'daggers drawn'?
That they are both arguing so fiercely the aggression may develop into a physical fight. The expression was first used in the sixteenth century, when people might, literally, be driven to draw their daggers against each other.

Damp squib
What is a 'squib'?
A squib is an explosive device, often used in pyrotechnics. When wet, it won't, of course, ignite – so a damp squib is something that was expected to be exciting but which turned out to be unsuccessful or just disappointingly uninteresting.

Dance attendance
Why do we say that a person who is at another's beck and call 'dances attendance' on him?
Because according to an old wedding custom, the bride on her wedding night was compelled to dance with and be attentive to every guest.

Dandelion
How did the 'dandelion' get its name?
It comes from the jagged edges of its leaves – which were supposed to look like a lion's teeth. The French form is *dent de lion* – that is, 'tooth of the lion'.

Darby and Joan
What is the reason we refer to a loving old couple as 'Darby and Joan'?
The expression comes from a ballad by David Woodfall in which Darby and Joan grow old together happily. Darby and Joan were real people; Woodfall actually served his apprenticeship with John Darby.

Dark horse
How did the phrase 'dark horse' get its present meaning?
At one time it was the practice among racing men for the owner of a well-known horse to disguise it by dyeing its hair in order to get better odds. Such a horse became a 'dark horse' – since you cannot make horsehair lighter by dyeing it. We say this now of a person about whom little is known, especially a competitor in a contest.

Davy Jones' locker
Where did the expression 'Davy Jones' locker' come from?
Jonah, the prophet of the Bible, was thrown into the sea. 'Jones' is merely a corruption of 'Jonah's'. 'Davy' is a corruption of the West Indian name for a 'ghost' or 'spirit' – *duffy*. So the phrase means 'the locker of the spirit of Jonah'. This is, of course, at the bottom of the sea.

Day of reckoning
How did the expression 'day of reckoning' originate?
The expression has been in use since the nineteenth century. The 'day of reckoning' is literally the day when you have to pay your bills, having reckoned up your accounts. It is used to mean the Judgement Day, or simply a decisive moment in your life.

Dead as a doornail
Why do we say something is as 'dead as a doornail'?
The doornail is the plate or knob on which the hammer of a door knocker strikes. Since this nail is knocked on the head many times a day, it cannot be supposed to have much life left in it. The related expression 'dead as a dodo' relates to the extinct bird and has been in use only since 1960 according to the *Oxford English Dictionary*.

Dead heat
Why do we call a race that results in a tie a 'dead heat'?
In trotting racing today, and at one time in almost all forms of horse racing, the horses had to run the course several times – two out of three or three out of five wins being needed. Each of these trials was called a 'heat'. If two horses tied in a heat the heat did not count – and was therefore called 'dead'. Today, we use 'dead heat' to mean any exact tie.

Dead men
How did empty liquor bottles come to be called 'dead men'?
A pun is intended. Empty liquor bottles are called 'dead men' because in both cases the 'spirits' have departed.

Dead ringer
Why is a person who strongly resembles someone else a 'dead ringer'?
A ringer was a counterfeit coin so convincing that it could only be detected if it made a loud ringing sound when dropped on a hard surface. Later, a ringer was a fast horse that bore a striking resembles to a nag with a poor racing record; this horse was replaced for the inferior one with high odds and then bet on, often resulting in huge wins. 'Dead' in this context means 'exact' and is added for emphasis.

Deadhead
Why is a person riding a railway train and paying no fare called a 'deadhead'?
The term comes from the theatre. A person admitted without having to pay any admission is called a 'deadhead', because he or she cannot be counted when the revenue is figured – since the dead cannot reach into their pockets to pay. The term is less appropriate when applied to railway travel; a dead body transported on a train, perhaps to his or her funeral, must have a ticket and also a live accompanying passenger – or at least pay double fare.

Deaf as an adder
What is the origin of the expression 'deaf as an adder'?
The basis for this simile is found in Psalm 58, which reads: 'They are like the deaf adder that stoppeth her ear; which will not harken to the voice of charmers, charming never so wisely.' It is to be surmised, therefore, that a person 'as deaf as an adder' is – or at least was originally – only as deaf as was convenient.

Dear John letter
When did the expression 'Dear John letter' originate?
During World War II. They were the letters sent to members of the armed forces by their wives or sweethearts breaking the news that the relationship was over. While it is never pleasant to write or receive one of these letters, it is to be hoped that they have not been superseded by the 'Dear John' fax, text or email!

Decide
Where does the word 'decide' come from?
The term comes from the Latin *decidere*, meaning 'to cut away' and one method of arriving at a decision is by eliminating all but one possibility – 'cutting away' all that is irrelevant.

Delirium
How did the word 'delirium' come to have its present meaning?
This Latin word originally meant 'to go out of the furrow in ploughing'. But since the thoughts of a person in delirium leave the beaten track and become jumbled, they too can be said to 'leave the furrow'.

Delta
Why is the mouth of a river named after the Greek letter 'delta'?
All the river deltas in the world are named after the delta of the Nile, so called because its triangular shape is the same as the letter *delta* – Δ.

Demijohn
Where did the jug we call a 'demijohn' get its name?
From the French. They called it a *dame-jeanne* (Lady Jane) because its shape and wickerwork covering seemed to give it the figure of a woman wearing an old-style corset – small at the waist but bulging above and below.

Derrick
Why do we call a crane a 'derrick'?
Because a famous seventeenth-century hangman of Tyburn, England was named 'Derrick'. Since he too hauled objects up by means of a rope and stationary arm, a crane ghoulishly came to be called a 'derrick'.

Dessert
How did the last course of a meal come to be called 'dessert'?
The word comes from the French *desservir*, meaning 'to clear the table'. At one time the cloth was removed before the final sweet was served: today, of course, we merely remove the crumbs of the previous courses.

Desultory
Where do we get the word 'desultory'?
From the Roman circus. The term literally means a 'rider of two horses' and the ancient Roman circus performers who rode two or more horses were apt to leap from one to another. So a person who is inconstant and who changes his position 'from one horse to another' is therefore said to be 'desultory'.

Deuce
What is the origin of the tennis term 'deuce'?
The term comes from the French *deux*, which means 'two'. In tennis it signifies that two consecutive points are needed by one or other side to win the game.

Devil's advocate
Why do we say a person who questions every statement in a discussion is playing the 'devil's advocate'?
It is because when any name is proposed for canonisation in the Roman Catholic Church, two advocates are appointed. One of these is called 'God's Advocate' and says all he can in support of the candidate; the other, 'the Devil's Advocate', says all he can against the candidate.

Devil's luck
Why is good luck called 'devil's luck'?
Because it was once believed that only the devil could bring you 'luck' in this world. Good people had to wait until they got to the next world for their reward. This is still believed by many.

Dexterity
How did 'dexterity' come to mean ability?
'Dexterity' literally means 'right-handedness'. The person who was right-handed was assumed to be able to do things with ease. The person who was left-handed would surely botch them up. For this same reason we use the French *gauche*, meaning 'left-handed', to describe an awkward person. We also use the Latin word for 'left' – *sinister*. We have changed this to mean 'evil', since signs seen on the left side were said to bring ill luck, while those seen on the right brought good luck.

Die is cast
Is the 'die' of the expression 'the die is cast' the kind used in casting metal?
No. The 'die' referred to is the singular of 'dice'. Once you have thrown or cast the dice, you cannot pick them up and throw them again.

Digs
Where did 'digs' as a synonym for 'lodgings' come from?
This is generally supposed to be a British term for 'lodgings', but it actually started during the days of the gold rush in California, where each man had his own 'diggings'.

Dinosaur
Why do we call someone who fails to adapt to change a 'dinosaur'?
There have been many attempts to explain why dinosaurs became extinct, but the most probable is that they simply failed to adapt to climate changes and other environmental factors. Therefore it is assumed that someone who refuses or is unable to adapt to changing circumstances is likely to suffer the same fate as the dinosaurs.

Dirt cheap
Why do we say this or that is 'dirt cheap'?
Because nothing is of less value. Should you gather a big pile of dirt you would not thereby increase your wealth; in fact you would probably have to pay someone to take it away.

Disgusted of Tunbridge Wells
Who was the original 'Disgusted of Tunbridge Wells'?
This was the pen name of a regular contributor to *The Times* letters page during the first half of the twentieth century. He specialised in contemptuous, ultra-critical attacks on organisations and individuals that in some way displeased him. He (or she) was never identified, but even after the contributions stopped the label has lived on, possibly because Tunbridge Wells is widely regarded as the epitome of self-satisfied Englishness.

Distaff side
Why are women of the family tree said to be on the 'distaff side'?
The female line of descent is so-called because the women of the household once spun the thread for their weaving using a 'distaff'. The male line of descent is called the 'spear side' because they did the fighting.

Dive
How did 'dive' come to mean a place of tawdry amusement?
A great many of the drinking places that specialise in such amusement are located in basements below street level – and many of their customers do not want to be seen entering them. Therefore, they 'dive' in.

Do as you would be done by
Who first coined the advice to 'do as you would be done by'?
Charles Kingsley, in his children's story *The Water Babies*. Tom, the subject of this moralising Victorian tale, is rewarded for good behaviour by Mrs Doasyouwouldbedoneby – but is also dealt the same unkind treatment he has given to others by Mrs Bedonebyasyoudid.

Dog days
Why are hot summer days called 'dog days'?
Because the ancient Romans believed that the six or eight hottest days of the summer were caused by the Dog Star, Sirius, rising with the sun and adding its heat to the day. They called these days *cuniculares dies* – 'dog days'.

Dog eat dog
Where did the expression 'dog eat dog' originate?
There is a Latin proverb 'dog does not eat dog' that suggests the exact opposite; but when behaviour has broken down completely and everyone is concerned only with themselves, all reason and rules are abandoned and it's 'dog eat dog'.

Dog in the manger
Where does the expression 'dog in the manger' come from?
The allusion is to the fable of a dog who lay in the manger on top of the hay and would not let the ox or horse eat – though the dog itself could not enjoy such food. It is used to describe someone who won't give to someone else something he cannot himself use.

Dog's chance
Why does someone with no chance have a 'dog's chance'?
The expression came into being in the nineteenth century. The 'dog' referred to in this instance is not a pampered pet or a fine hunting hound but a street mongrel – considered to be pretty much the lowest of the low. There was no possibility that such a cur would ever rise from this miserable position – so a person having little chance of success doesn't have a dog's chance.

Dog's life

Has a 'dog's life' always been an easy life?
No. In the sixteenth century, when the expression was first used, it meant the opposite. The dog would have been a stray, constantly struggling to survive life on the streets. In the twenty-first century, when most dogs have a good life, the expression is more often used ironically to describe a pleasurably lazy existence.

Dogwatch

What is the reason the late afternoon watch on board ship is called the 'dog watch'?
The term was originally 'dodgewatch' and the watch was created so that the same men would not have to serve at the same time day after day. Each half of the crew served a 'dogwatch' between four in the afternoon and eight in the evening. It was a two-hour shift rather than a four-hour shift; and so the two groups of men changed the hours during which they were on watch from day to day.

Doh-Re-Mi-Fa-So-La-Te-Doh

Did the syllables used to verbalise the notes of the scale ever have any meaning?
Yes. When Guido d'Arezzo invented his hexachord scale, he took the first syllables of a part of a hymn to St John as the names of his notes – since each line of this hymn began a note higher:
Ut *queant laxis*
Resonare fibris
Mira gestorum
Famuli tuorum
Solve polluti
Labii reaturm.
'Doh' was later substituted for 'ut' because it sounded better. With the invention of the octave, a name for the seventh note was needed. It was taken from the initial letters of the last line of the hymn:
Sancte **I**ohahannes
At an even later date, 'te' was substituted for 'si' for ease in singing.

Doing a bunk

Why do we say a person who ducks responsibility is 'doing a bunk'?
Because a soldier anxious to get out of an unpleasant detail will pretend illness and lie in his bunk.

Dominoes

How did the game of dominoes get its name?
The monks of the French monastery who invented the game gave it its name. The winner was expected to recite the first line of the vesper service, '*Dixit Dominus, Domino, Meo*'. 'Domino' is just a shortened form of this line.

Done to a turn

Why is a meal that's cooked to perfection 'done to a turn'?

This description originates from when meat was cooked by being turned on a spit over a fire.

Don't care a fig

Where does the expression 'don't care a fig' come from?

The 'fig' here is not the fruit but the Italian *fico*, which in French is *figue*. The Italian *fico* is a contemptuous gesture made by thrusting the thumb between the index and middle fingers of the same hand.

Don't count your chickens

Where does the expression 'don't count your chickens before they're hatched' come from?

The allusion is to the fable of the market woman who began figuring how much money she would get for her eggs. Then with this money she would buy this and that and continue to make a profit until she had made a fortune. She was still figuring her profits when she accidentally kicked over her basket of eggs and broke them. The saying reminds us not to make plans too far into the future as something down the line may go wrong.

Don't shoot the messenger

Why was the messenger in danger?

The first recorded version of this plea was made by Sophocles ('No one loves the messenger who brings bad news'). Shakespeare later used it in both *Henry IV, Part II* and *Antony and Cleopatra*. An invisible code of conduct in warfare demanded that an emissary, or messenger, sent to the enemy side was returned unharmed. The phrase is used today as a reminder that it is not the bearer of the bad news who should be blamed for a bad state of affairs. A variation – 'Don't shoot the piano player. He's doing his best' – was spotted by Oscar Wilde in a saloon bar in Leadville, Colorado, USA.

Dope

Why is a simpleton called a 'dope'?

Because he generally acts as though he were drugged. When opium is heated, it flows sluggishly and 'dope' comes from *doop*, the Dutch word for a thick liquid.

Double cross

Where did we get the term 'double cross'?

From prize fighting. The fighter who intentionally loses a fight 'crosses up' the spectators and those who have bet on him to win; if he wins after he 'crosses up', his manager and those who have bet on him lose. These two 'cross ups' make a 'double cross'.

Double-header
What is the origin of the baseball term 'double-header'?
It was taken from the railways, where a double-header is a train with an engine at each end. Hence, in baseball, a 'double header' is two games played on a single afternoon.

Double whammy
Where does the expression 'double whammy' come from?
From the world of sport in 1940s America, when a whammy was the word used to describe a curse on a player or the game itself. 'Double whammy' followed shortly afterwards to mean one factor that creates two problems.

Doubting Thomas
How did a person who doesn't believe anything get the name 'Doubting Thomas'?
The expression is an allusion to the Thomas of the Bible – 'one of the twelve, called Didymus' – who refused to believe it was Christ who had risen from the dead until he felt the wounds.

Dough
Why is money called 'dough'?
Just as English public schoolboys visited the baker's shop near the school, so American children went to the ice-cream parlour to buy cakes, pies and puddings. The boys' nickname for these delicacies – especially pudding – was 'dough'. And, since they spent their pocket money on 'dough', they came to call the money itself 'dough'.

Doughboy
What is the origin of 'doughboy' as a nickname for a soldier?
The name 'doughboy' was originally given to a small cake or dumpling supplied to British sailors. It was later applied to British infantrymen – since they would apply pipe clay whitening to parts of their uniform and so became covered with 'dough' when it rained.

Dovetail
How did we come to say that things which fit together well 'dovetail'?
The allusion is to furniture making. In putting furniture together with mortice and tenon joints, the tenon is cut with a spread that looks something like a dove's tail.

Down in the dumps
Why are you 'down in the dumps' when dejected?
'Dumps' may be derived from Swedish *dumpin*, meaning melancholy, Dutch *dompig*, damp, or German *dumpf*, gloomy. People have been 'down in the dumps' since the early sixteenth century, possibly even earlier as a ballad of 1475 has the line 'I wail, as one in doleful dumps'.

Down a peg

Why do we say when we have lessened a person's dignity that we have 'taken him down a peg'?

The expression may have had its origin in the tuning of stringed instruments – but it gained meaning from a custom of the British Navy. The height of a ship's colours or flag was once regulated by the pegs to which the line was fastened on deck. The ship's colours were raised in saluting a visiting dignitary – and the higher they were raised the greater the honour. So, to take the ship colours down a peg is to decrease the honour – and to take someone 'down a peg' is to lower his dignity.

Downsizing

What does it mean when a company is 'downsizing'?

'Downsizing' is corporate-speak for reducing the workforce. The company may use the term to indicate that this is a streamlining measure to make the company more efficient, but for the victims of downsizing, it's just another word for redundancy. A later variant is 'right-sizing' (which probably still doesn't fool anyone).

Draconian measures

What is it about 'Draconian measures' that make them so severe?

Draco was a particularly exacting seventh-century BC Athenian lawmaker, who reformed the city's legal code and constitution. He also put them in writing for the first time so that the law could no longer be interpreted arbitrarily. The laws were harsh: for example, any debtor whose status was lower than that of his creditor was forced into slavery, and execution was frequently the penalty for fairly minor crimes. However, Draco's laws did distinguish between murder and involuntary homicide. Interestingly, Draco died of suffocation when he was smothered by hats, shirts and cloaks thrown on his head – by his admirers.

Dragoon

What is the origin of the word 'dragoon'?

The soldiers known by this name once carried short muskets. These muskets spouted fire like dragons and so the muskets were called 'dragons' and the men who carried them became known as 'dragoons'.

Draw in one's horns

Why do we 'draw in our horns' when we economise?

It's an allusion to the snail, which draws in its body, including its horned tentacles, when disturbed. There isn't much opportunity to spend from inside a shell.

Drawing teeth

What do we mean when we say that something is like 'drawing teeth'?

Though extracting teeth is undoubtedly painful, the expression is most often used to describe something that is excruciatingly protracted such as a boring speech.

Dressed up to the nines

How did we come to say that a very smartly dressed person is 'dressed up to the nines'?

The expression comes from the Old English dialect form 'dressed to the eyne' – meaning 'to the eyes'. A person dressed up to the nines is up to their eyes in clothes.

Dressing down

Why is a reprimand called a 'dressing down'?

A butcher preparing beef for market takes a knife and slashes the animal's carcass. This is called 'dressing down' the beef. Similarly, a person receiving a tongue-lashing is said to receive a 'dressing down'.

Drink like a fish

Why do we say a person 'drinks like a fish'?

Since fish don't actually drink, this is something of an odd expression. It came into use in the seventeenth century because fish appear to swallow water continuously, though in fact they are pushing it out over their gills to extract the oxygen.

Drop of a hat

Why does 'at the drop of a hat' mean immediately?

Races used to begin when the starter dropped a hat or, sometimes, a handkerchief. When it hit the ground, this was the signal for everyone to start – immediately.

Drop on him

Where did 'have the drop on him' get its meaning of having the advantage on someone?

In the Wild West the usual procedure in shooting a pistol was to point it at the sky and then drop the forearm until the pistol pointed at its victim. When two gunmen met, the first to drop his forearm to the firing position 'had the drop' on the other.

Drum up trade

How did we get the expression to 'drum up trade'?

It was once the custom for a salesman upon reaching a town to beat a drum or ring a bell to attract the attention of the community. Having drawn a sufficient crowd, the salesman would tell his news and sell his merchandise.

Drunk as a fiddler

What is the reason we use the phrase 'drunk as a fiddler'?

The expression refers to the fiddler at weddings and wakes, whose fee was often set at 'all the liquor you can hold'. In order to get his full fee it was necessary for him to drink long and often.

Dry goods
Why are 'dry goods' so called?
Dry goods are so called to differentiate them from the goods sold by a greengrocer. The greengrocer sells things that are wet – or, at least, juicy.

Ducks and drakes
Where did we get the expression 'playing ducks and drakes' to mean careless spending?
From a childish game called 'ducks and drakes' in which the children toss stones – sometimes without very good aim. So anyone who throws his or her money about is playing 'ducks and drakes' with it.

Dude
What is the origin of the word 'dude'?
'Duds' are our clothes – from the Middle English word *dudde* meaning 'to dress'. The Easterner who goes West dresses himself in fancy 'duds' – and to Westerners seems to pose or strike an attitude. The word 'Dude' is 'dud' plus attitude.

Dukes
Why are a person's fists called his 'dukes'?
Because the Duke of Wellington had a very large nose; men with large noses were therefore called 'dukes' and later their noses were given this name. A hand doubled into a fist became a 'duke buster'; then 'buster' was dropped and fists became 'dukes'.

Dull as dishwater
How did we get the expression as 'dull as dishwater'?
The term was not 'dishwater' originally, but 'ditch water'. Ditch water is stagnant and there will be nothing of interest to an angler in it. Fishing in ditch water is, threfore, certainly dull.

Dutch
Why do we use 'Dutch' in so many negative ways?
Because there was a time when Great Britain and Holland were bitterly competing for foreign commerce and mastery of the sea. The British used the word 'Dutch' as a term of opprobrium and disparagement and to assert their own superiority. The following are typical examples of this use:
Beat the Dutch
Only a person who told a completely incredible story could ever hope to 'beat the Dutch'.
Dutch auction
This term refers to an auction that opens with a high bid and then works downwards.
Dutch bargain
This phrase has two meanings – a bargain concluded over drinks and a one-sided bargain that is no bargain at all.

Dutch concert

The allusion is to the great noise and uproar made by a party of Dutchmen in various stages of intoxication – they sing, they quarrel and they shout.

Dutch courage

By this we really mean courage excited by drink. The British claimed that the only way the captain of a Dutch man-of-war could instil in his men sufficient courage to fight, was to set up an open hogshead of brandy.

Dutch reckoning

When a bill that is disputed grows larger, that is 'Dutch reckoning'.

Dutch treat

No treat at all; everyone pays for themselves.

Dutch wife

This name for a bolster was based on the presumption that Dutch women were poor bed companions – as unresponsive as the open frame bolsters used extensively in the Dutch Indies for resting the legs while in bed.

In Dutch

The phrase just means 'in disgrace'.

My old Dutch

This synonym for wife was coined by the famous English music hall performer, Albert Chevalier, who explained it by saying: 'A wife's face resembles that of an old Dutch clock.' His choice of 'Dutch' rather than some other nationality was undoubtedly influenced by the general disparaging use of the word.

Dyed in the wool

Why do we say that someone who has very fixed ideas about something is 'dyed in the wool'?

Because when woollen cloth is dyed the colour may not be even throughout; but if the dye is applied to the wool before it is spun and woven, all the cloth will be exactly the same shade.

Eager beaver
Why is an industrious person an 'eager beaver'?
This common expression is used to describe someone who is as busy and hardworking as the animal itself. Beavers are renowned for the speed and efficiency with which they construct dams, both for their habitation and to preserve their water supply.

Eagle eyed
When did we first describe a highly observant person as 'eagle eyed'?
The phrase has been used in this context since the early nineteenth century, no doubt because an eagle can see its prey from great distances above ground. It may also derive from a legend that has existed for as long as there have been written records in English. When its eyes dull with age, an eagle will fly upwards and look at the sun's rays, which then burn away all the cloudiness.

Eagle has landed
What do we mean when we say the 'eagle has landed'?
In July 1969, Neil Armstrong signalled the successful landing of the lunar module, *Eagle*, on the surface of the moon. The expression has come to be used at the successful accomplishment of any difficult task.

Ear to the ground
What is the derivation of the expression 'keeping your ear to the ground'?
It comes from the American Indian tradition of listening to the ground to detect the approach of horses through the vibration of their hooves. This may, however, just be an invention of Hollywood westerns. It is applied to someone who keeps constantly alert to what is going on.

Early bird
What is an 'early bird'?
This now usually means someone who wakes early and performs at their best in the morning. The original expression – 'the early bird catches the worm' – meant that the first person to arrive would gain an advantage.

Ears are burning

When our 'ears are burning', why do we believe someone is talking about us?

The ancient Romans paid particular attention to burning or tingling in various bodily organs. Such sensations in the left ear signified evil intent from outside influences; in the right that the person was being praised or would receive good fortune. They also believed that a twitching right eye foretold a visit from a friend.

Easy as ABC

Why do we say something easy is as 'easy as ABC'?

Because the schoolchildren of early England, given a hornbook and told to read from it, found the first part of it the easiest – for then they only had to read off the letters of the alphabet. There is no easier reading.

Easy as duck soup

What is the reason we say a task is as 'easy as duck soup'?

A pond or puddle of water is, by humorous analogy, called 'duck soup'. A puddle caused by rainfall will materialise without human effort. Thus 'easy as duck soup' describes a project requiring no special effort.

Easy as pie

Why do we say an uncomplicated task is as 'easy as pie'?

Because the full expression is 'as easy as eating pie' – and eating pie is generally considered to be a pleasant, entirely trouble-free occupation.

Eat one's head off

What is the reason we say a lazy person 'eats his head off'?

The expression was originally applied to horses whose food cost more than they could earn. It refers to the fanciful notion that a horse eating oats will keep on nibbling its lips after the oats have gone and, if not stopped, will finally succeed in eating off its own head.

Eat your heart out

Has 'eat your heart out' always been said by a victor to annoy the loser?

No. This usage is fairly recent. There was an ancient belief that sorrow or envy would eat away at the heart, and by the beginning of the twentieth century it was an established term for pining.

Eavesdropper

How did we get the term 'eavesdropper'?

In Saxon times in England, the owners of estates could not build their homes or cultivate their land right up to the property line. They had to leave a little space for the drip from the eaves. This space soon came to be called, from that fact, the 'eavesdrip'. An 'eavesdropper' was a person who placed himself in the 'eavesdrip' to overhear what was being said.

Economy
Where does the word 'economy' come from?
From the Greek word for 'house manager'. The one place where we generally insist on the careful expenditure of money is in our own home.

Egg on
Does 'egg on' have anything to do with eggs?
No. The origin is an ancient Scandinavian word from which 'edge' also derives. 'Edge' can mean 'sharpness' or 'urgency', which links with the meaning of the expression – to encourage or urge.

Egg on your face
Why does being foolish give you 'egg on your face'?
People used to throw eggs or rotten fruit at bad performers and unfortunate wrongdoers clamped in the stocks. It has come to mean looking foolish and being derided for something you have done.

Eggs in one basket
What do we mean by 'don't put all your eggs in one basket'?
If you put everything of value in one place that turns out to be not safe at all, then you will have lost everything. This saying means, in effect, spread the risk.

Electricity
Who invented the word 'electricity'?
Dr William Gilbert – who became physician to Queen Elizabeth I in 1601. Dr Gilbert gave the name 'electric' to static electricity produced by rubbing a piece of amber with a cloth. He derived the name from *elektron*, the Greek word for 'amber'.

Eleven, Twelve...
How did the numbers 'eleven' and 'twelve' and the 'teens' get their names?
Eleven comes from 'leave one' – you count the ten fingers and that leaves one. Twelve is 'twa' or 'two left'. 'Thirteen' is 'three plus ten'... and so on.

Ethnic cleansing
When was 'ethnic cleansing' first used as a euphemism for genocide?
The term has certainly existed in Russian (*etnicheskoye chishcheniye*) since 1988, but it became infamous in 1991 when used in a *Times* interview in reference to the Serbo-Croatian conflict.

Etiquette
What is the origin of the word 'etiquette'?
At one time visitors to the court of France who might not know how to behave properly were given a card of instructions – a ticket of sorts. From this the French devised the term 'etiquette' and applied it to all rules of social behaviour.

Every dog has his day
What do we mean by 'every dog has his day'?
That even the most downtrodden person will at some time have the upper hand. The medieval Dutch scholar Erasmus believed the saying evolved from the circumstances of the death of Euripides; the illustrious Greek playwright was fatally mauled by a pack of dogs in 405 BC.

Examine
How did we come to use the word 'examine' to mean 'test'?
An old-fashioned balance scale has a little indicator on it, in order to show which tray outbalances the other. This indicator was called in Latin an *examen*. Thus, to 'examine' is to watch this indicator and, by analogy, 'weigh in the balance'.

Exception proves the rule
What is the origin of the expression the 'exception proves the rule'?
Originally the word 'prove' meant 'test'. And so the phrase merely means that the 'exception tests the rule'. In this sense the saying is quite logical.

Expletive deleted
What do we mean by 'expletive deleted'?
That rude or offensive words have been replaced by an asterisk or a euphemism. The phrase was originally used in the transcripts of the Watergate tapes in 1973.

Eye for an eye
Did 'eye for an eye' originate in the Bible?
Yes. The Old Testament law of punishment 'eye for eye, tooth for tooth, hand for hand, foot for foot' is in the book of Exodus. However, this harsh decree was revised by Christ in the Sermon on the Mount: 'Ye have heard that it hath been said, An eye for an eye, and a tooth for a tooth. But I say unto you, That ye resist not evil' (Matthew 5: 38–9).

Eye of a needle
What is the reason we say that something is as difficult as 'for a camel to pass through the eye of a needle'?
The expression comes from the Bible. 'The needle's eye' was a name given to a small gateway built in the wall of Jerusalem for the use of pedestrians. A small camel could actually work its way through this gate – if it knelt down and struggled hard – but it would be very difficult.

Faction

Where did we get the word 'faction'?

From the Romans. The charioteers who performed in the Circus Maximus were divided into four different parties and the Latin word for 'party' is *factio*. Each factio wore a different colour and originally represented a different season of the year – though in time the number of factions was increased to six. Civil war between the 'blues' and the 'greens' in AD 532 led to the current meaning of 'opposing political groups'.

Fag end

Does 'fag end' have anything to do with smoking?

Not originally. The last part of a piece of cloth was made of coarser material than the rest and left hanging loose. 'Fag' seems to be a corruption of 'flag' – meaning 'hang down'. It became a term to describe the last and poorest part of anything, which included the stub of a cigar and later a cheap cigarette.

Fall guy

Why do we call a sucker a 'fall guy'?

The word 'fall' not only means to 'stumble' but also to be 'lured' or 'entrapped'. We call a person a 'fall guy' who is entrapped and left to suffer the punishment, while the one who did the actual mischief escapes.

Fall on your sword

Does 'fall on your sword' derive from Japanese hara-kiri?

Yes. A noble samurai would prefer honourable suicide by ritual disembowelment to surrender. In addition, a disgraced Roman of Imperial times might be offered the opportunity to kill himself, or indeed herself, with their own sword rather than face execution – falling on it being perhaps less awkward to manage and having a guaranteed outcome. These days we use the expression figuratively when someone pre-empts disgrace or capture by resigning or taking other action.

Famous for fifteen minutes
Who coined this term to describe transitory celebrity status?
The expression and the concept was the creation of the American artist Andy Warhol. It disparages not only the celebrity, but the commercial opportunism of the media and the short-lived attention span of the public. Warhol's original statement was: 'In the future, everyone will be world-famous for fifteen minutes'; later he deliberately confused interviewers with variations such as 'In the future, fifteen people will be famous' and 'In fifteen minutes everybody will be famous'. Perhaps very recently it has developed a gentler use – that everyone deserves and might achieve their moment in the spotlight.

Farce
How did the word 'farce' come to mean 'comedy'?
'Farce' comes from the Latin *farcire*, meaning 'to stuff'. The early miracle plays were padded or stuffed with jokes and low comedy scenes – and so this type of comedy came to be called 'farce'.

Fart in a spacesuit
Who first coined the expression 'as welcome as a fart in a spacesuit'?
The Glaswegian stand-up comedian Billy Connolly. He said that he once opened a show for Elton John – and this was how wanted the audience made him feel.

Fast and loose
Why is a person indulging in trickery said to be playing 'fast and loose'?
'Fast and loose' was the name of one of the 'skin games' played at fairs in England in the Middle Ages. The trickster folded a belt and then asked a player to pin it fast to the table with a skewer. After the player had done this the trickster suggested a bet. Then he loosed the belt and showed all that it had not been pierced by the skewer anywhere.

Fat's in the fire
Why do we say the 'fat's in the fire' when we mean there is trouble ahead?
Because if fat is spilled from a frying pan into the fire, the flames leap up and can burn you.

Feather in your cap
Where did we get the expression a 'feather in your cap'?
The Native American who added a new feather to his headgear for every enemy slain was the father of this phrase. The same procedure has been followed by many other races and nations. A feather in your cap is an achievement to be proud of.

Feeding frenzy
What animal gave rise to the phrase 'feeding frenzy'?
Sharks. When they congregate at a source of food they can attack even each other in their anxiety to feed. From the late 1970s it has been used to mean furious commercial competition.

Feet of clay
What do we mean when we say someone has 'feet of clay'?
That even those who appear to be important may be just as ordinary as the next person. The phrase has a Biblical origin: King Nebuchadnezzer dreamed of a statue finished at the head in gold and from there downwards in materials of diminishing value. The statue is gradually destroyed until nothing is left standing but the clay feet. Daniel interpreted this dream as a vision of Nebuchadnezzer's declining kingdom.

Fiasco
How did a complete failure come to be called a 'fiasco'?
The making of a fine Venetian glass bottle is a difficult process for it must be perfect. If, in blowing, the slightest flaw is detected the glassblower turns the bottle into a common flask – called in Italian, *fiasco*.

Fiddlesticks
Why do we use the exclamation 'fiddlesticks'?
In the eyes of the serious-minded to 'fiddle' is to waste time – as in the term 'fiddling around'. The fiddle is, therefore, a worthless object. Since the bow or 'fiddlestick' is even less important to fiddling than the fiddle itself, 'fiddlesticks' means that something is of no worth whatsoever.

Fifth column
What is the origin of the term 'fifth column'?
This phrase was coined by the Spanish Fascist General Emilio Mola. While Franco's forces were besieging the city of Madrid, Mola made a special broadcast to the Loyalists defending the city in which he stated: 'Four of our columns are marching upon your city and at the appropriate time a "fifth column" behind your own lines will rise to the attack.'

Filibuster
How did we get the name 'filibuster' for legislative obstruction?
The Spanish called a freebooting pirate out to get what he could for himself a *filibustero*. A legislator with similar ideas was also given this name. The usual method employed for this purpose by the legislator was to obstruct the passage of all bills until his demands had been met. So today any legislator who obstructs legislative procedure is said to 'filibuster'.

Filthy lucre

Has 'filthy lucre' always been just a rather unpleasant way of saying 'incredible riches'?

No; the phrase has softened over time. *Lucre* meant money, in a negative connotation, from the fourteenth century and appears in that context in the works of Chaucer. It described monetary gain that had been achieved unfairly or at the expense of others. Even nowadays there is a hint of disapproval in the expression.

Final straw

What is a 'final straw'?

The full proverb, which has been in use since the seventeenth century, is 'it's the final straw that breaks the camel's back'. The 'final straw' may in itself be only trivial, but following a series of other negative occurrences, it's the one that makes everything too much to bear.

Fine Italian hand

Why do we use the expression 'fine Italian hand'?

This phrase has a double meaning. In the fifteenth century Italian penmanship was exceedingly fine and ornate; at the same time the court politicians of Italy were exceedingly sly – and so the term was used to mean 'sly manipulation covered by beautiful appearance'.

Fingers crossed

Why do we cross our fingers when hoping for good luck?

To make the sign of the cross, thus warding away evil.

Fire and water

How did we come to say a person who suffers trial and tribulation goes through 'fire and water'?

Because in early times a method of proving one's innocence was to suffer trial by ordeal. One ordeal was by fire; the person either walked barefoot and blindfolded through hot coals or carried a red-hot iron bar for a distance. Another ordeal was by water; the person plunged his or her hand into a pot of boiling water.

Firedogs

Why do we call andirons 'firedogs'?

Because at one time real 'dogs' were placed in a wheel cage at one end of a roasting spit and had to run round and round the wheel to turn the spit. Sometimes a live coal was placed inside the wheel to speed up the dogs.

First blush

How did the phrase 'at first blush' come to mean without full consideration?

Because it is to be presumed that the first time a young lady is presented with a proposition – either honourable or dishonourable – she will naturally blush. So, 'at first blush' means immediately and without any previous consideration.

Fish needs a bike

Who coined this feminist slogan?

The full saying is 'a woman needs a man like a fish needs a bicycle' – in other words, men are superfluous to women's needs. It has been attributed to various feminist writers, but the self-confessed originator was Irina Dunn, a distinguished Australian educator, writer and politician. She was paraphrasing in 1970 the words of an earlier saying: 'Man needs God like a fish needs a bicycle.'

Fishwife

Was a 'fishwife' just the wife of a fishmonger?

No. A fishwife was a working woman in her own right, though this occupation was not considered to be particularly reputable. Fishwives sold fish from baskets along the quays, advertising their wares of necessity at the top of their voices, hence the negative connotations concerning their vocal force and dubious vocabulary.

Fit as a fiddle

What is the reason we say someone is as 'fit as a fiddle'?

The phrase was originally 'fit as a fiddler' and referred to the stamina of fiddlers – who could play all night long without ever getting tired.

Flak

What is the origin of the word 'flak'?

It is a contracted form of the German '*Fliegerabwehrkanonen*' – meaning 'anti-aircraft gun'. Since allied airmen came more closely in contact with its missiles than the gun itself, they used 'flak' to mean the barrage the gun sent up.

Flame

How did the word 'flame' come to mean the object of our affections?

Just as in our popular songs 'June' is often rhymed with 'moon', the common rhyme of the French classics is *flamme* and *âme*. So we call the loved one (*âme*) a '*flamme*'.

Flapper

Why were young girls in the 1920s called 'flappers'?

Because a fledgling wild duck flaps its wings but cannot fly. A young girl was said to be a flapper when she attempted to act like a woman but was not yet one.

Flash in the pan

Why do we use the expression 'flash in the pan' for something that disappoints?

The old flintlock type of gun had a 'pan' on which a little trail of powder led from the charge in the gun to the flint. When the hammer struck the flint and ignited this trail of powder but the gun did not go off – then it was just a 'flash in the pan'.

Fleshpots
What is the reason carnal desire is called 'hunger after the fleshpots'?
'Fleshpots' were originally pots in which the flesh of animals was cooked – and 'to hunger after the fleshpots' was to want a good meal of meat. Only by analogy did the flesh become human.

Flibbertigibbet
How did the word 'flibbertigibbet' come to mean a restless chatterer?
By the addition of several unnecessary onomatopoeic syllables to make the meaning doubly clear. 'Gib' is no doubt a variant of 'gob' which means 'mouth'; 'flibber' is an echoic variant of 'flutter'. So a flibbertigibbet is a 'flutter-mouth'.

Flivver
Where did the term 'flivver' to describe an old, small or cheap car come from?
From a confused blending of 'flopper' and 'fizzler'. The word was widely used in the early part of the twentieth century. It isn't heard so much these days, despite the fact that it would describe perfectly the very first cars so many of us owned!

Flotsam and jetsam
What is the difference between 'flotsam' and jetsam'?
Flotsam is found floating in the sea: jetsam has been thrown overboard (or jettisoned) into the water. In general usage, the two words are combined to denote odds and ends.

Flush
Why is a person with plenty of money said to be 'flush'?
Because a container filled to the top is filled 'flush'. Likewise, a pocket filled to the top with money is flush – and so is its owner.

Fly a kite
How did the expression 'go fly a kite' originate?
In England many years ago, a person who sent begging letters to wealthy men whom he knew only by name – in a general sort of hope that some one of them might come to his rescue – was said to be 'flying kites'. The expression was prompted by the fact that you can, by flying a kite, see how the wind is blowing. So, to tell a person to go fly a kite was the equivalent of saying, 'ask someone else – not me'. Later, the meaning became 'go play by yourself' – and from this comes the use of the term as a euphemism for a far more vulgar expression.

Fly off the handle
Why do we say a person 'flies off the handle' when he gives vent to his anger?
The expression refers to the head of an axe. A woodchopper giving vent to his anger might chop so violently that the head of his axe could 'fly off the handle'.

Flying Dutchman
What is the reason a vessel vaguely seen passing in a fog is called a 'flying Dutchman'?

According to legend, the *Flying Dutchman* was a vessel that started to round the Cape of Good Hope, the southernmost tip of Africa, during a bad storm. When the crew became frightened and mutinied, the captain put the ringleaders to death. Then the Holy Ghost, in the form of St Elmo's fire, appeared at the masthead and told the captain to desist. He answered by drawing his pistol and firing at the light – but the pistol exploded in his hand and paralysed his arm. The captain was wild with rage; he cursed and swore he would continue to round the Cape against the wind if it took him until 'the crack of doom'. The Creator took him at his word – and ever since then the ship may be seen sailing against the wind in a vain attempt to round the Cape of Good Hope.

Fogey
How did a man who is behind the times come to be called an old 'fogey'?

There was once a standard English word, 'foggy', which meant 'fat' or 'bloated' or 'moss-grown'. The Scottish adopted the word as 'fogey' and used it as a disrespectful name for an old man who was behind the times.

Forlorn hope
Why do we say a hope that is likely to come to nothing is 'forlorn'?

The usual sense of 'forlorn' is miserable, lonely or forsaken but in this context it means 'faint'. This was originally a Dutch expression, *verloren hoop* or 'lost troop' and was applied to those soldiers who were most likely to be killed.

Four-in-hand
What is the reason 'four-in-hand' can describe both a kind of coach and a kind of tie knot?

The coach is drawn by four horses and all the reins are held by one person – in just one hand while wielding the whip with the other. The ends of the tie hang from the throat in a manner similar in appearance to the reins falling down from the hand of the four-in-hand driver.

Freedom suit
What is the origin of the term 'freedom suit'?

In colonial times, men of means in America paid for the passage of Europeans who wished to come to the New World; they exacted, in return, a period of indentured service. At the end of this period of servitude the master gave his indentured servant a 'freedom suit', which followed the style of the period and had none of the distinguishing features of the livery previously provided.

Freelance
Why is an independent writer, photographer or the like called a 'freelance'?
A medieval mercenary soldier who was free of any continuing loyalties was known as a 'free companion'. Sir Walter Scott in his novel *Ivanhoe*, coined a more descriptive term for such a soldier – 'free lance'.

Freudian slip
What is a 'Freudian slip'?
It's the inadvertent remark or mispronunciation that is believed to reveal what one really thinks. The expression has little psychological foundation, though it does reflect Sigmund Freud's belief that the unconscious is the reservoir of suppressed desires.

Friend in need
What is a 'friend in need'?
The original proverb from which this comes – 'a friend in need is a friend indeed' – goes back to the third century BC. It might be taken that it is the friend who is in need, but actually it is someone who stays your friend during *your* need. The proverb means that you can truly trust those who stand by you when you are in trouble.

Frog
Why is a Frenchman called a 'frog'?
Because the shield of Paris has frogs on it and because French cuisine includes the delicacy frogs' legs – which the English once considered to be very perplexing indeed.

Full of beans
How did we come to use the term 'full of beans' to describe an active and energetic person?
Beans have long been considered an energy-giving food. Therefore, a lively person must be full of beans.

Full blast
Why do we call the utmost 'going full blast'?
Furnaces in steel plants use a forced draught of air that is called a 'blast' – and the furnace is called a 'blast furnace'. When in full operation the furnace is 'going full blast'.

Full monty
What does the 'full monty' mean and where did it come from?

The phrase became widely known because of the hit 1997 film of the same name, though it had been used earlier – possibly from the 1950s. It just means 'the whole lot'. There is almost an embarrassment of suggestions for its possible origin: it may be a variation of 'the whole shebang' or of 'the full amount'; a reference to wool bales imported from Montevideo; gambling slang, either for the kitty in the card game *monte* or from Monte Carlo casinos, where the expression would mean 'breaking the bank'; a reference to Field Marshal Montgomery's partiality to a full English breakfast; or the distinction between buying a two-piece or a three-piece suit from the British tailors Montague Burton – splashing out on the waistcoat as well would be going for the 'full monty'.

Funny bone
Why is the spot at our elbow called a 'funny bone'?

It is a pun. This spot not only gives us a 'funny' tingling feeling when we hit it; it is also located at the enlarged end of the bone whose medical name is the humerus.

Gag
How did a joke come to be called a 'gag'?
The term was originally used by actors to mean an ad-lib joke thrown in to flummox another actor. The joke would stop his next lines as effectively as a gag.

Game's not worth the candle
What does it mean if the 'game's not worth the candle'?
That an activity is not worth the trouble or cost involved. The reference is to a gambling session in which the amount of money at stake amounts to less than the price of the candle needed to illuminate the game.

Gamut
Why do we say a person 'runs the gamut' of emotions?
Because 'gamma' represented the last note on Guido d'Arezzo's musical scale and 'ut' represented the first note used in his singing scale (it was later replaced by 'doh'). So, to 'run the gamut' has come to mean to run the entire scale of emotions.

Garble
Where does the word 'garble' come from?
From the Arabic word for 'sieve' – *ghirbāl*. At first 'garble' meant 'to sort out' and was applied to the selection and sorting out of individual passages from a man's writings. But the persons who made the excerpts often edited and changed the context considerably; and so 'garbled' came to be applied to words that were mixed up and mutilated.

Gargoyle
How did 'gargoyles' get their name?
'Gargoyle' is an Old French word that literally means 'throat'. Gargoyles were originally used as projections from the gutter of a building to carry the rainwater clear of the walls and they spurted this rainwater through their 'throats'.

Gat

How did we come to call a revolver a 'gat'?

The name 'gat' was originally applied to a machine gun invented by Dr Robert Gatling and first used during the American Civil War. But this gun had a cluster of ten barrels that looked something like the chamber of a revolver – and so the name was transferred to the revolver.

Geronimo

What is the reason American paratroopers shout 'Geronimo' as they jump?

Several members of the first unit of parachute troops formed at Fort Benning, Georgia, USA, went to see the motion picture *Geronimo*. Afterwards, in derisive reference to the mock heroics of their practice jumps, they started calling each other by this name. From this grew the paratrooper's practice of shouting 'Geronimo' as he leaps from the plane.

Gerrymander

How did we get the word 'gerrymander'?

The Democrat Elbridge Gerry was Governor of Massachusetts in 1812, with a Democratic legislature serving with him. In order to ensure increased representation in the State Senate, they carefully restructured the state so that the Federalist minority would not be able to elect a true percentage of the legislature. The painter Gilbert Stuart saw a map hanging in the office of Benjamin Russell, editor of the *Columbian Centinel*, and noticed the particularly irregular outline of one district. He added a head, wings and claws to it and exclaimed: 'That will do for a salamander.' 'No,' said Russell, 'Gerrymander.' Thus, to redistribute a state to give the maximum possible representation for one party at the expense of the other, came to be called 'gerrymandering'.

Get one's goat

Where does the term 'get one's goat' come from?

From horse racing. Racing men will often place a goat in the stall with a nervous race horse. The horse soon becomes accustomed to having a goat there and finds it comforting; it becomes less nervous and is not so easily upset. If, however, the owner of a rival horse can steal or 'get' the goat, then the horse is even more nervous than before and may lose the race.

Ghost walks

Why do we use the expression 'the ghost walks today' to mean it's payday?

Because of a theatrical anecdote. There was once a company of English strolling players who had been unpaid for some time. During a rehearsal when Hamlet said, in reference to the ghost: 'Perchance 'twill walk again', the ghost answered, 'No, I'll be hanged if the ghost walks again until our salaries are paid.'

GI
How did American soldiers get the nickname 'GI'?
'GI' stands for 'Government Issue' and the term was originally applied only to those articles that were actually issued by the government. But in army slang it now means practically everything in army life that is standardised, orderly or regimented – including the soldiers themselves.

Gift horse
What is the reason we say 'don't look a gift horse in the mouth'?
It is because the value of a horse is determined primarily by its age; and the age of a horse is determined by looking at its teeth. You should not question the value of something that is given to you – and you won't if you 'never look a gift horse in the mouth'.

Gild the lily
Why is it unnecessary to 'gild the lily'?
The lily is a thing so beautiful in itself that it needs no further embellishment. The source is a misquotation from Shakespeare's *King John*: 'To gild refinèd gold, to paint the lily.../Is wasteful and ridiculous excess.'

Gingerbread
Why do we call fancy scrollwork and gilt decorations 'gingerbread'?
Because at one time very fancy gingerbread animals sold at fairs were elaborately decorated with gilt or gold leaf.

Give the needle
Where did we get the expression 'give the needle'?
The term comes from a tailor's practical joke. When a group of tailors are sitting at a table side by side, one tailor will take his or her needle and slyly jab another in the rear. The startled reaction of the victim of this practical joke is considered by some to be highly amusing.

Go to pot
Why do we say that something that has deteriorated has 'gone to pot'?
It is because smiths generally keep a pot on hand into which they throw broken pieces of the metal on which they are working (though these scraps are ultimately melted down and used again so they aren't totally beyond rescue).

Gone for a burton

Does 'gone for a burton' have anything to do with Burton's beer?

It might have, but there have been numerous other suggestions for its origin. These include: seafaring sources – the complicated pulley arrangement called a Spanish burton, and burton being the name of a stowing arrangement across the ship's hold rather than fore and aft; a reference to being fitted for a wooden suit (that is, a coffin) at the tailors Montague Burton; rhyming slang for the British brewing town Burton-on-Trent – 'went', therefore 'gone'. However, it became widely known in World War II as a slang term for when a pilot met his death in the air, the derivation is fairly likely to be the RAF: 'burnt 'un' for an aircraft going down in flames; or the pilot who had crashed in the sea was 'in the drink' (had gone for a beer). Nowadays we apply the phrase to someone or something that is missing, broken or destroyed.

Gone west

How did 'gone west' come to be a way of saying someone has died?

In the beginning this expression just meant someone had disappeared from sight. In the early days of America many men who were wanted for a crime in the East, 'went out West' into the wilderness. Some lived, some died; but all who wished to do so disappeared from sight. But, since they might as well be dead, the term in time came to mean exactly that.

Good footing

Where does the expression 'on a good footing with the boss' come from?

During the reign of King Henry VIII of England the size of a man's shoe indicated his rank. An unimportant man wore a small shoe: an important man wore a large shoe to indicate that he was in good standing – 'on a good footing' – with the King.

Good innings

Why do we so often say that someone who has died had a 'good innings'?

There seems to be almost as many cricket-related sayings as seafaring ones. A cricketer has a good innings when he stays on the field a long time and scores many runs. So, too, someone who has had a pleasant, long life has had a 'good innings'.

Goose step

What is the origin of the term 'goose step'?

The name 'goose step' was originally applied to a British military exercise. A new recruit was made to stand on one leg and swing the other backward and forward without bending the knee, just as a goose stands on one leg and swings the other. Because of a similarity of appearance – in particular the straightened knee – the term was applied to the German military march step, in which the leg is raised sufficiently high to give a twenty-inch stride.

Gordian knot

How did a great difficulty come to be called a 'Gordian knot'?

This expression grew out of a legend about the Phrygian king Gordius. Gordius was a peasant who, upon being chosen king, dedicated his wagon to Jupiter and then tied the yoke to a beam with a rope made of bark. The knot was so intricate that it was said that whoever could untie it would reign over the whole East. Alexander the Great was shown the knot and told the story. 'Well, then', said he, 'this is how I do it' – and with his sword he cut the knot in two.

Gossip

Where did the word 'gossip' come from?

In early times a godparent of a child was called a *God-sibb* – *sibb* meaning 'related'. Since godparents were usually chosen from among distant relatives who met only at rare intervals, there was sure to be a great exchange of news and small talk at the christening. That led to the general belief that *god-sibbs* were idle chatterers – and to the adoption (and adaptation) of their name as a synonym for idle talk.

Gout

What is the origin of the word 'gout'?

'Gout' comes from the French *goutte* and literally means 'drop'. This disease was once supposed to be caused by the blood 'dropping' harmful material in and around the joints.

Grandfather clock

How did the 'grandfather clock' get that name?

The name comes from a popular song of the 1880s that began:
  'My grandfather's clock was too tall for the shelf
  So it stood ninety years on the floor.'

Grapefruit

Is there any reason why 'grape' is used in preference to another fruit in the word 'grapefruit'?

Yes. Grapefruit grow on the trees in clusters like grapes.

Grapevine

Why do we say a rumour travels via the 'grapevine'?

The term is a shortened form of 'grapevine telegraph'. In 1859 Colonel Bernard Bee constructed a telegraph line between Placerville and Virginia City by attaching the wire to trees. In time the wire slackened and lay on the ground in loops that resembled wild trailing grapevines. During the American Civil War, similar lines were used by troops and since the reports that came in over such 'grapevine telegraph' lines were more often that not conflicting, the term 'grapevine' was used to refer to widespread rumours with no definite source and that were generally false.

Grass widow

What is the origin of the term 'grass widow'?

In the days before divorces the only proper husbandless mother of a child was a widow, while a girl who took up prostitution as a profession was said by country folk to have 'gone on the turf' or 'gone on the grass'. If such a girl became the mother of a child, she would naturally claim to be a widow – although 'wed in the grass and widowed there'. Nowadays the term is applied to a woman whose husband is temporarily away, whether on business or some leisure pursuit.

Greek meets Greek

Where did we get the expression 'when Greek meets Greek'?

The reference is to the wars of Alexander of Macedonia. He set out to conquer the other states of Greece, but each in turn responded with obstinate resistance. An early play about Alexander the Great contains the line: 'When Greeks joined Greeks then was the tug of war.'

Greeks had a word for it

Why do we say 'the Greeks had a word for it'?

Because the words of classical Greek had many forms – a fully conjugated verb possessed several hundred. This variety of word forms made possible a precision in expression not attained in any other ancient language – or in many modern ones.

Greenhorn

How did we come to call an inexperienced person a 'greenhorn'?

The word was first applied to a young ox with new horns. By analogy these new horns were 'green' ('greenhorn' in this sense was used as long ago as 1460.) Since a person who does not know his way about is like a young or greenhorn ox that doesn't know which way to turn when you shout 'gee' or 'haw' at it, the term 'greenhorn' has been applied to the person.

Gretna Green marriage

Where is the Gretna Green of the term 'Gretna Green marriage'?

In Scotland. Although England has long had rather strict marriage laws, at one time Scotland did not. All the marriage ceremony needed in Scotland was a mutual declaration by the two elopers in front of witnesses. So English boys and girls went to Scotland to be married in a hurry – and to Gretna Green in particular, since it was the nearest and most accessible spot over the Border. There they had only to declare their intent to become legally married, without licence, banns or a priest.

Grocer

What is the origin of the word 'grocer'?

The word originally meant a wholesaler. An English merchant who dealt in spices, dried fruits, tea, coffee and such foodstuffs in retail amounts was called a 'spicer'. A wholesale dealer in these articles was called a 'spicer en gross' – or a 'grosser' – since he sold goods in bulk and by the gross. 'Gross' is from the French *gros*, meaning great or large.

Grog

Why is the rum served on British naval ships called 'grog'?

Because Admiral Edward Vernon of the British navy was nicknamed 'Old Grog' – in reference to the grogram cloak he always wore. (Grogram is a coarse silk fabric mixed with wool and stiffened with gum.) As an economy measure, Vernon introduced into the navy the custom of serving rum mixed with water instead of undiluted rum. This mixture was called 'grog' in his honour – and the name stuck.

Guy

What is the reason the word 'guy' is used to mean a man?

The British use 'guy' to signify a grotesque and ludicrous person – in allusion to Guy Fawkes, a leader of the Gunpowder Plot of 1605, and the effigies of him that used to be strung up on street corners on 5 November. The American term is derived from the 'guy' rope of a circus tent – in such phrases as 'Who's the "main guy" here?'.

Gymnastics

Where did we get the word 'gymnastics'?

The word comes to us from the Greek *gumnos*, which means 'naked'. From this the Greeks devised the word *gymnasium* to denote a public place for athletic sports. The athletes of early Greece removed their clothes to compete with one another.

Gyp

Why do we call a trickster a 'gyp'?

The word comes from the Greek and literally means 'vulture'. Students at Cambridge University applied the name to the servants allocated to them by the college, since these servants found innumerable ways of obtaining tips from them and so, by implication, preyed upon them like vultures. From Cambridge the word went into general use – a person who was not quite honest and his method of acquiring things by trickery both being called a 'gyp'.

Gypsy

How did the gypsies get their name?

Their name derives from Egypt, which the gypsies claim as their original native land. But it is far more likely that they originally came from India in the Middle Ages – and they merely passed through Egypt on their way to Europe.

Hair of the dog

Why is a morning-after drink as a hangover cure called taking a 'hair of the dog'?

Because the ancients believed that one of the best cures for rabies, or any other disease you might obtain from a dog bite, consisted of taking a 'hair of the dog that bit you' and placing it in the wound.

Halcyon days

How did 'halcyon days' come to mean a peaceful and pleasurable period of time?

The original 'halcyon days' were 15 days in the spring – the seven days preceding the vernal equinox in March, the day itself and the seven days following it. This is the brooding time for the halcyon, or kingfisher, and since its nest was believed to float on the sea, the superstition arose that calm weather always prevailed at this time of year.

Half-cocked

Where does the expression 'go off half-cocked' come from?

From hunting. A gun at half-cock is in the safety position; it cannot be fired. But a hunter may, in his excitement at sighting game, raise the gun to his shoulder and pull the trigger while still 'half-cocked'. Nothing happens. And so, to go off half-cocked means to attempt something in a hurry without proper preparation and to fail in achieving the end.

Half-seas over

Why do we say an intoxicated person is 'half-seas over'?

It's a nautical phrase and originated with the thought that a ship that is half-way across the sea will keep on going rather than turn back. But the application of the expression to an intoxicated person was strengthened by a pun – for the English imported from Holland a strong beer that the Dutch called *op-zee-zober*, meaning 'overseas beer'.

Halloween
How did 'Halloween' come to be so called?

The old Celtic calendar began on 1 November and, therefore, 31 October was New Year's Eve – the night on which witches and hobgoblins rode about for one last fling. With the introduction of Christianity, the old New Year's Day became 'All Saints' Eve' or 'All Hallows' E'en'. Though the name was changed, the customs – and the belief that witches rode on this night – have persisted to this day.

Ham actor
Why is a poor actor called a 'ham'?

This theatrical slang term, contemptuously applied to low-grade actors, is a shortening of the term 'hamfatter'. It comes from the old-time blackface comedian's practice of putting ham fat on his face so that it would be easy for him to remove the burnt cork after the show. All 'whiteface' actors once looked down on 'blackface' comedians.

Hammer and tongs
How did we come to use the phrase 'hammer and tongs' to mean energetically?

The allusion is to the vim and vigour exhibited by a blacksmith showering blows with his hammer upon the molten iron taken from the forge fire with his tongs.

Handicap
Where does the word 'handicap' come from?

The word comes from the usual procedure in drawing lots. Slips of paper are placed in a hat or 'cap' and each person in turn draws one out by placing his 'hand i' the cap'. This practice is still followed in drawing for position in a horse race. Slips bearing the names of the horses are drawn from a hat and the first horse drawn gets the position next to the rail, the second horse gets the adjacent position, and so on.

Handkerchief
What is the origin of the word 'handkerchief'?

The 'ker' of this word comes from the Old French *covrir*, meaning 'to cover'. The 'chief' comes from *chef*, meaning 'head'. A 'kerchief' was originally a head covering, in particular the piece of cloth used by women to cover their heads when entering a Catholic church. A 'handkerchief' was one carried in the hand.

Hang fire
What is the reason a delayed action is said to 'hang fire'?

It is because a flintlock gun does not always go off immediately. Though the spark has been set, the powder in the pan may fizz for a while before exploding the charge behind the shot.

Hangout
How did 'hangout' come to mean a gathering place?
'Hangout' originally meant a place of business – for at one time almost all professional men, artisans and tradespeople hung out signs at their premises to advertise their business. The term had its origin in the phrase 'where do you hang out your sign?'.

Happy as a clam
Why do we use the expression 'happy as a clam at high tide' to mean extreme happiness?
Because clams appear to desire nothing more than to be left alone. Since clams are gathered only when the tide is out, they should be at their happiest at high tide.

Happy as Larry
Who was Larry and what was he so happy about?
There are two possible sources for this expression that describes being as content as it is possible to be. One is that it originated from the nineteenth-century Australian boxer Larry Foley, who instigated boxing wearing gloves rather than fighting bare-knuckled. This improvement must have given him a certain happy glow. The other possibility is that it comes from English dialect, either *larrie*, meaning joking or jesting, or *larrikin*, a naughty youth.

Hard and fast
Why do we say that something inflexible is 'hard and fast'?
It's a nautical term applied to a grounded ship. 'Hard' means firm and 'fast' means fixed.

Hard-boiled
Does being 'hard-boiled' have anything to do with eggs?
No. The allusion is to boiling cloth, especially for millinery purposes, to make it stiff and hard. A hard-boiled person is thick-skinned and not easily offended – they may even be insensitive.

Hard up
What is the origin of the slang expression 'hard up'?
It was originally a nautical term. To put the helm 'hard up' is to put it as far as possible to windward – in order to turn the ship's head away from the wind. So today, one who has very little money and must turn away from any financial storm is said to be hard up.

Harp on things
How did the term 'harping' come to mean the reiteration of a single point?
To 'harp' is really to play the harp; and the allusion is to an old saying, 'Harping on just one string' – in other words, playing the same note over and over again.

Harrier

How did cross-country runners get the name 'harriers'?
A dog that is used to chase hares is called a 'harrier' – and the first cross-country runs were made by men playing the game hare and hound.

Harum–scarum

What is the origin of the term 'harum-scarum'?
Hare is an old English verb meaning 'to excite' or 'to worry' – we use it in 'harass'. The term 'harum-scarum' originally meant to 'scare 'em' and 'worry 'em'.

Haul over the coals

Why do we call a thorough questioning or reprimand being 'hauled over the coals'?
Because at one time, those suspected of heresy were literally hauled over the coals of a fire in order to induce them to confess their sins and adopt the true faith.

Haywire

How did the word 'haywire' come to be used to describe something that's in a mess?
The term seems to have first become popular in the logging camps of the four north-eastern US states known as the North Woods. In distant camps, the teamsters would save the wire from the bales of hay to use for various repairs; cooks would string haywire above the stove to dry clothes and hang up ladles – and often use it to bind the stove together. In time, a camp that was notoriously poor in its equipment came to be known as a 'haywire' camp; from this usage the term has come to mean broken, sick, crazy and a score of other things, none of them praiseworthy. The term now commonly means 'mixed up' – like a pile of haywire after it's been removed from the bales.

Hearse

What is the origin of the word 'hearse'?
The word literally means a 'harrow' which was a device for breaking up soil – the Old French for 'harrow' being *herse*. The harrows of that time were triangular – the same shape as the frames used to hold the candles set at the head of a coffin. Even today, triangular frames are used in Catholic churches to hold the candles burning before the statue of a saint. Because this candle rack was shaped like a harrow, it too was called a *herse*. Then, since the frame used to carry the coffin from the house to the church had candles on it, this frame, in turn, was named a *herse*. When carriages were substituted for the frame used to carry a coffin they took the same name – 'hearse'.

Heart of gold

What does it mean if someone has 'a heart of gold'?
That the person is fundamentally good, though his or her virtues are often hidden by more evident faults.

Heart on one's sleeve
How did we get the expression 'wearing one's heart on one's sleeve'?
From chivalry. It was the custom among the knights of old to tie a kerchief, scarf or other favour from a lady on their sleeves. Since this indicated the state of a man's heart he was said to wear his heart on his sleeve.

Heater piece
Why is a triangle of land called a 'heater piece'?
Because it looks like a flatiron or 'heater'. For the same reason, the building erected on the 'heater piece' at Fifth Avenue and Twenty-third Street in New York City is called the 'Flatiron Building'.

Heeled
Why is a person who is well prepared or in funds said to be 'well-heeled'?
The term comes to us from the cockpit. A fighting cock has artificial steel gaffs attached to its legs in place of its own spurs. A 'well-heeled' bird is one whose fighting gaffs are efficient and effective.

Held in abeyance
What is the reason we say that something delayed is 'held in abeyance'?
The French word *bayer* means 'to gape'. 'Abeyance' literally means 'hold your mouth open' and the allusion is to those who, while waiting for something to happen, stand with their mouths open.

Hell for leather
How did we come to use the expression 'hell for leather' to describe a fast, reckless drive or ride?
The original phrase was 'all of a lather', and it was used to describe the state of a horse that had been ridden fast and hard. However, the expression didn't seem strong enough, so this intensification was devised to give a greater suggestion of recklessness.

Hep
Where did 'hep' get the meaning 'well-informed and up to date'?
In the army. A drill sergeant, in counting the rhythm for his marching men, will call out 'Hep! Hep!' – a shortening of 'Step! Step!'. The rookie who has learned to 'keep in step' (both literally and figuratively) with his companions is 'hep'. From this we get the present meaning to describe a person who knows his way around.

Hermetically sealed
Why do we say that something that is airtight is 'hermetically sealed'?
Chemists were the first to use an airtight seal. In order to keep air out of a bottle they heated the neck of the bottle until it was soft and then twisted the glass until the opening was sealed. Chemists were once called 'Hermes' – after the mythical alchemist Hermes Trismegistus – and so 'hermetically sealed' means 'sealed by the chemists' method'.

High and dry
Is 'high and dry' a nautical metaphor?
Yes. A ship that is beached or on the rocks is left 'high' by the receding tide and will eventually become 'dry' once out of the water. We say someone is 'high and dry' when they are stranded and defenceless.

High horse
What is the reason a haughty person is said to be on his 'high horse'?
The horseman has long considered himself superior to those on foot. If the horse is tall, he's just that much more superior.

High jinks
How did we come to call fun and frolic 'high jinks'?
'High jinks' is a variant of 'high pranks', the name of a once-popular game that combined dice and charades – the fall of the dice determined which member of the group should pretend to be some fictitious character. Of course, playing the game led to general letting down of the hair – 'high jinks' as we say today.

High seas
What is the origin of the expression 'high seas'?
By 'high seas' we mean all the waters that are not the property of a particular country – that is, those beyond the 12-mile (previously 3-mile) limit. The word 'high' is used to indicate that the seas are public, just as 'highway' means a public way. In both cases, of course, 'high' also means chief or principal.

Hippopotamus
Where did the 'hippopotamus' get that name?
The name comes directly from two Greek words – *hippos* and *potamós* – and literally means 'river horse'.

Hit it off
Why do we say two people who get on well together 'hit it off'?
To 'hit it off' in hunting originally meant to 'strike the scent'. Two people who find they have something in common 'hit the scent' and are off!

Hitch
What is the reason a temporary setback is called a 'hitch' in our plans?
The 'hitch' in our plans is like the 'hitch' that develops when a horse becomes lame. The word is Scottish and means 'motion by jerks'. If we set out on horseback and our horse develops a limp, we can't arrive in time and there's a 'hitch in our plans'.

Hobby

How did a leisure pursuit come to be called a 'hobby'?

A plough horse is called 'Dobbin', 'Robin' or 'Hobin'. From this latter we get the diminutive 'hobby', meaning 'a small horse'. 'Hobby' is used in this sense to refer to a child's toy or 'hobby horse'. A toy horse just furnishes amusement – it cannot be worked – so an occupation pursued for amusement and not as work is a hobby.

Hobnob

Why do we say two people in intimate conversation are 'hobnobbing'?

The term was once spelled 'habnab' and its meaning was 'have and not have'. As a synonym for 'give and take', it's an apt description of an intimate conversation.

Hobson's choice

Where did we get the expression 'Hobson's choice'?

From Tobias Hobson, who kept a livery stable in Cambridge, England, in the seventeenth century. Hobson let out his horses only in rotation, saying, 'This or none'. 'Hobson's choice' means no choice at all.

Hocus–pocus

Why do we say 'hocus-pocus' when doing a magic trick?

Because of the wizard Ochus Bochus of Scandinavian mythology. He did all sorts of tricks and 'hocus–pocus' is just a corruption of his name.

Hoe–cake

How did the 'hoe-cake' get that name?

It came about because in pioneer homes this Indian corn bread was often baked on the broad, thin blade of the hoe used in the cotton fields.

Hoi polloi

Who are the 'hoi polloi'?

Literally 'the many'. This Greek term is used to mean the majority or the masses, though rarely in a flattering way.

Hoist by one's own petard

We often say this, but where does it come from and what is its exact meaning?

This is an age-old expression – Shakespeare uses it in *Hamlet*: 'For tis the sport to have the engineer hoist with his owne petar.' A petard was a gunpowder-filled weapon of war used to blow openings in gates or walls. In effect they were the forerunners of bombs. 'Hoist' in this context means to raise, to lift, or to blow up. So to be hoist by one's own petard is to be harmed by one's own scheme.

Hold a candle
Why do we say that an inferior person cannot 'hold a candle' to a superior one?
In the Roman Catholic Church, a candle is held or placed before the image of a favourite saint when praying to that saint for a special favour. A person who cannot hold a candle to another – that is, who cannot even pray to him or her – is indeed inferior.

Hold the fort
Why, when we assume responsibility, do we 'hold the fort'?
This expression has been traced to an order by General Sherman in 1864: 'Hold the fort at all costs, for I am coming.' It has two meanings: to assume responsibility in a superior's absence; and to keep a situation secure, the fort being a castle or stronghold.

Hone your skills
What do we do when we hone our skills?
A honing stone was used to sharpen a blade. So, to 'hone our skills' means that we practise and improve them, to 'sharpen' our abilities.

Honeymoon
Why do we call the period that immediately follows a marriage a 'honeymoon'?
The 'honey' alludes to the sweetness of marriage delights; the 'moon' to the rapidity with which it wanes.

Hooch
Where did we get the word 'hooch' as a synonym for strong drink?
From Alaska. When America acquired Alaska in 1867, a small body of troops was sent into the territory. Since the soldiers were forbidden to bring any alcoholic beverages with them, they set up their own stills and brewed a very powerful drink from sugar and flour. The Alaskan natives called this drink *hoochinoo* – the name by which it was known until the gold rush to the Klondike; then *hoochinoo* was shortened to 'hooch'.

Hoodlum
How did a ruffian come to be called a 'hoodlum'?
It's all due to illegible handwriting. In an attempt to coin a name for a San Francisco gang, a newspaper reporter took the name of the gang leader, Muldoon, and reversed it – making it 'Noodlum'. The typesetter couldn't read his writing and set it up as 'Hoodlum'.

Hook and ladder
Why is the fire truck that carries ladders to the fire called a 'hook and ladder'?
Because in times past – and even today – a ladder topped with a hook was used by firemen in scaling a building. This hook on the end of the ladder gave the name to the fire apparatus.

Hoosegow
How did a jail get the name 'hoosegow'?

The term comes from the Spanish word for 'judged' or 'sentenced' – *juzgado*. The 'd' is not pronounced by Mexican peons, so the words sounds almost exactly like 'hoosegow'. A peon found guilty of a crime seldom had enough money to pay a fine, so almost inevitably served a jail sentence. Because of this, a Mexican would explain his absence from an American's ranch by saying *juzgado*. The American, knowing the peon had been to jail, assumed the term meant 'jail' – and so came to call a jail a hoosegow.

Hoot
Why do we use the expression 'I don't give a hoot' to show our unconcern?

A 'hoot' is, of course, a shout of derision and contempt. A person so unconcerned that he doesn't even care to 'give a hoot' in derision is, presumably, totally uninterested.

Hopping mad
How did the phrase 'hopping mad' come to stand for extreme anger?

Because if you're angry enough, you will use not only your tongue and your hands to express your emotion but also your feet – and then you'll be 'hopping mad'.

Hopscotch
Does the 'scotch' in 'hopscotch' mean the game had Scottish origins?

No. The 'scotch' just means 'scratch'. In playing the game you must hop over the lines scratched in the ground.

Hornbook
What is the reason the 'hornbook' was given that name?

The early primers of England were made of a thin board on which were printed the alphabet, the digits and the Lord's Prayer. This was covered with a thin sheet of cow horn to keep it from becoming soiled.

Horse latitudes
How did the 'horse latitudes' get that name?

The region of calms between 30 degrees and 35 degrees north latitude got the name 'horse latitudes', because ships laden with horses and cattle for America and the West Indies were often becalmed there for so long that the horses died.

Horse sense
What is the sense referred to in the expression 'horse sense'?

The allusion is not to the intelligence of a horse, but to the shrewdness of horse traders.

Horseradish
Why is the 'horseradish' so called?
'Horse' is often used to mean 'coarse', as in 'horse mackerel' and 'horse bean'. The 'horse radish' looks something like the common radish but has a far coarser texture – and stronger flavour.

Horses for courses
What do we mean by 'horses for courses'?
That people's skills should be matched to the task in hand. Different horses race better under different conditions of the course.

Hotchpotch
Why is a mixture of a little of this and a little of that called a 'hotchpotch'?
A hotchpotch, or 'hodgepodge', is a stew or hash made up of whatever ingredients are to hand.

How do you do?
Why do we greet people with 'how do you do?'?
The last 'do' means 'fare' and we're really asking: 'How are things going?'

Hubba-hubba
How did 'hubba-hubba' come to be chosen as the modern 'wolf call'?
In much the same way as the word 'barbarian' came to be adopted. The ancient Greeks felt that foreigners spoke in nonsense syllables – their languages sounded like a series of 'ba-ba' sounds to them – and so they called foreigners 'barbarians'. In like manner, the American soldier in the Pacific during World War II considered the native languages, as far as he was concerned, just so much 'hubbub'. Basing his choice on this word, he picked two nonsense syllables of his own to call out when seeing an attractive native girl – 'hubba-hubba'.

Humble pie
Why do we say an apologetic person eats 'humble pie'?
It's a pun. The entrails of deer are called 'umbles' and at one time they were made into a pie to feed the servants and huntsmen of a lord – while the lord and his guests ate the meat on the carcass. So a person who humbled himself was said to 'eat humble pie'.

Hunky-dory
How did we get the expression 'everything's is hunky-dory'?
From the Low Dutch word *honk*, meaning 'safe'. The word was also used to mean a 'goal' in a game – and so a man who scored or who safely reached base in a game such as baseball was said to 'honk' or 'be honky'. 'Dory', quite possibly, comes from 'all right'. When everything is hunky-dory, everything is fine.

Hurrah

Who were the first people to shout 'hurrah'?

The Prussians first used this word as a battle cry in the War of Liberation of 1812. The German interjection, *hurrâ* comes from *huren*, meaning 'to rush'. But many other nations use similar words as a battle cry.

Hussy

Why is an unpleasant or immoral woman called a 'hussy'?

The word is just a corruption of 'housewife' and originally had no unkind implications attached to it, although for many years it was not applied to a married woman.

Idiot

Has the word 'idiot' always meant a mentally deficient person?

No. The word is Greek and at first an 'idiot' was just a private citizen who held no public office. However, since the Greeks considered it a great honour to hold office, the word finally came to mean a person who couldn't take part in public affairs.

In at the death

What is the origin of the term 'in at the death'?

In fox hunting it was considered very desirable to keep up with the dogs – or at least to have arrived by the time the trapped fox was killed. We use the expression to describe being present at the conclusion of events.

In the groove

Why do we say a musician's improvisations are 'in the groove'?

The allusion is to the phonograph record and needle. When the needle is 'in the groove', the music sounds fine: when it is out of the groove, it's terrible.

In the red

Why is being in debt being 'in the red'?

Before bank statements were generated by computer, overdrawn balances were printed in red. Someone who spends more than they have is therefore 'in the red'.

In the swim

Where do we get the expression 'in the swim'?

From fishing. Anglers call a gathering of fish a 'swim'. The term was eventually applied to social gatherings at which people came together in large groups. So, to be 'in the swim' is to be part of such gatherings.

Inaugurate

What is the reason we say we 'inaugurate' a man when he is installed in office?

The term is from the Latin *inaugurare* which means 'to take omens from the flight of birds'. No Roman official was installed without the approval of the birds.

India rubber
Where did 'India rubber' get this name?
The same mistake that led Columbus to think he had reached India when he discovered America, led to people calling rubber 'India rubber'. Columbus reported that on his second voyage he found the natives of Haiti playing a game with 'balls made from the gum of a tree'.

Indian giver
Why is a person who gives someone a gift and then expects to receive something in return called an 'Indian giver'?
At one time the traditions of Indians were not understood. An Indian who gave a gift would, in keeping with the Asian courtesy of reciprocal giving, expect something in return. A Westerner would unfairly consider the Indian to be more interested in gain than in being generous.

Indian summer
How did a warm spell in late autumn get the name 'Indian summer'?
Since the term 'Indian' was once used generally to indicate something sham or bogus, the sham summer of late autumn came to be called an 'Indian summer'.

Infantry
What is the origin of the word 'infantry'?
The term comes from the word 'infant' – since this part of the army was originally made up of the page boys of the knights.

Inside track
Where did we get the expression 'he's got the inside track'?
From horse racing. The best position for a horse, the shortest to the ultimate goal, is the one nearest the rail – the 'inside track'. So having the inside track means having the advantage.

Irons in the fire
What is the origin of the expression 'too many irons in the fire'?
The allusion is to the blacksmith, who generally keeps several pieces of iron in the fire, in order to have one always ready for his anvil. But if he has too many in the fire at the same time, he can't watch them all for when they need attention.

Ivory tower
Why is someone not connected with reality in an 'ivory tower'?
The tower suggests shelter and isolation; ivory implies chastity and naivety. Ivory, while hard, is also brittle and would make a highly impractical construction material. The expression usually has negative connotations, implying that the occupier of an ivory tower is so deeply drawn into study that he or she cannot connect with those outside. 'Ivory tower' in Latin is *turris eburnean* – one of the names for the Virgin Mary.

Jack Robinson

What is the origin of the expression 'before you can say Jack Robinson'?
There are several explanations of this phrase, but the best story is of a fickle gentleman-about-town named Jack Robinson. Robinson used to go calling on his friends and would then change his mind and leave before his name could be announced.

Jalopy

How did the 'jalopy' get that name?
An old and dilapidated automobile rides more like a horse than a smooth-running modern car; the motion is 'gallop-y' and from this we get, by a softening of the 'g', 'jalopy'.

Jam session

Why is a gathering of musicians playing together without scores called a 'jam session'?
It's because all of the musicians – who are playing for their own amusement – 'jam' or crowd as many notes as possible into a bar of music, as each in turn improvises.

Jazz

Where does the word 'jazz' come from?
The word comes to us from Creole French – by way of 'Mr Jasbo', the minstrel show dandy who carried a cane and wore spats. In Creole French, a 'dandy' is called a *chasse beaux* – or a 'beaux chaser' – because he's so attractive that he chases all the other beaux away. The music we now call jazz was used in the 'cakewalk' – a form of competition for these beaux at social gatherings. Minstrel shows adopted the character, the dance, the music, the name of the dance and the name *chasse beaux* for the competitors – but, not knowing French, spelled the latter, 'Jassbo' and 'Jazzbo'.

Je ne sais quoi
What does it mean when someone has a certain 'je ne sais quoi'?
Obviously, this is not an English expression, but it is so often used that it deserves explanation here. The literal translation from French is 'I don't know what', and we use it to say that something, or more often someone, has a special quality that you can't quite define.

Jeep
Why is a 'jeep' called that?
The first quarter-ton reconnaissance cars delivered to the US Army had painted on their sides the letters 'G.P.' – which stood for 'general purpose'. 'G.P.' when said quickly became 'jeep'. The utterance of a character in the Popeye comic strip of Elzie Crisler Seagar, 'Eugene the Jeep' – who confines himself to saying, 'jeep, jeep, jeep' – may have helped to popularise the word.

Jerry-built
How did a poorly built house come to be called 'jerry-built'?
'Jerry' comes from 'jury' and 'jury' is from the Old French word *ajurie*, meaning 'relief'. The term is similar to the nautical 'jury mast' or 'jury rig' – a temporary mast or rigging set up when a ship's regular mast and rigging have been carried away by a storm. Hence a 'jerry-built' house is one that is not built to last.

Jerusalem artichoke
Has the 'Jerusalem artichoke' any connection with the city of Jerusalem?
Only through an error. Jerusalem artichokes are members of the sunflower family and the Italian word for sunflower is girasole. The artichoke's name is just a corruption of this word.

Jitterbug
Where did the 'jitterbug' get its name?
From the bugs themselves – those little bugs you see scooting about on the surface of still ponds in the spring. The appropriateness of the term is reinforced by the meaning of 'jitter' – 'to act in a nervous manner' – and the fact that 'bug' is a name for an enthusiast.

Jive
Why are 'jive' music and dancing called that?
To 'duck and dive' is a term applied to square dancing – one of the calls being 'Duck for the oyster; dive for the clam'. Similarly, and in apposition to this, modern athletic dancers 'jump' and – for alliteration – 'jive'.

Jobsworth
What is a 'jobsworth'?

It's a fairly modern description of someone who acts in a deliberately obstructive way, by excessively exercising their job description. The epitome of the jobsworth is someone employed as a menial public service officer who, despite having little authority, takes care to wield as much power and cause as much inconvenience as he or she possibly can.

Jog the memory
What is the reason we say we 'jog the memory'?

'Jog' really means 'shake', and when we 'jog' a person's memory we shake it up. Likewise, a 'jog trot' is a shaking trot.

John Bull
Why is the name 'John Bull' used to represent England?

The 'Bull' is an allusion to the British fondness for beef – just as a Dutchman is called 'John Cheese'. But a Scottish satirist, Dr John Arbuthnot, published in 1712 a pamphlet that popularised the term. It was entitled *The History of John Bull* and in it Dr Arbuthnot named his characters after animals. He called the Frenchman 'Lewis Baboon', the Dutchman 'Nicholas Frog' and the Englishman 'John Bull'.

Josh
What is the origin of the word 'josh'?

The Scottish dialect 'joss' means 'to jostle' or 'push against'. This word – influenced by the name of the American humorous writer Josh Billings – gave us the present word and its meaning 'to push around humorously'.

Jot
Why do we say 'not a jot' and 'I don't care a jot'?

The 'jot' referred to here is the Greek letter 'iota' – which was often written merely as a dot below a long vowel. When written thus, it was the smallest of all Greek letters.

Jug
How did a jail come to be called a 'jug'?

Originally a 'jug' was not a prison but a pillory or 'stock'. The word comes from the French *joug*, meaning 'yoke'. When the pillory was abolished and prisoners were transferred to jail, the name 'jug' was transferred with them.

Juggernaut
Why are tanks, trucks and other large vehicles called 'juggernauts'?

The god Vishnu, one of the Hindu trinity, has a thousand names. One of these is *Jagannatha*, meaning 'Lord of the World'. In Hindu mythology Vishnu owns a vehicle that is 45 feet high and has 16 wheels, each of which is 7 feet in diameter. So, any big vehicle on wheels is called a juggernaut.

Juke box
Where did the 'juke box' get that name?

The more ecstatic religious revival meetings in the South of the USA produce a sort of frenzy characterised by rhythmic jumps and jerks. When in such a state a person is said to 'juke' – from a combination of the two words. Dancers, under the stimulation of extremely 'hot' music, will likewise 'juke'; music that produces this state is 'juke music' – and so, since the coin machine phonograph specialises in this type of music, it is called a 'juke box'.

Jump the gun
Why do we 'jump the gun' when we act prematurely?

This expression comes from athletics, where a gun is used to start a race. If we 'jump the gun', we gain an unfair advantage by starting before the permitted time.

Jump over the broomstick
What is the origin of the expression 'she jumped over the broomstick'?

A woman who started living with a man without any marriage ceremony generally ignored housewifely duties – pots, pans and the broomstick. So, she was said to 'jump over the broom'. It's interesting to note that the phrase sired a custom; women entering into such a relationship would, instead of allowing themselves to be carried over the threshold of their new home, jump over a broomstick into it.

Junket
Why is the dessert 'junket' called that?

The Italians called bulrushes *giunco*. They served a cream or curd cheese on a mat made from these leaves – and so called the cheese *giuncata*. From this the English derived the word 'junket' – which first meant a curded cream cheese served with spices, but is more often nowadays applied to the milky jellied dessert.

Kangaroo
How did the kangaroo get its name?
Captain James Cook, who discovered Australia, asked the tribesmen of the Endeavour River region the name of the animal. They answered, 'kangaroo'. Whether that was the name of the animal itself or just an answer signifying 'I don't know' (or maybe even 'Go away and leave us alone') is something we don't know.

Kangaroo court
Why is a mock trial held by convicts called a 'kangaroo court'?
The term originated in Australia at the time when it was a penal colony. The use of 'kangaroo' is an allusion to the prisoners' belief that they had no more say about what happened to them than the kangaroos.

Keelhaul
What is the reason a severe reprimand is called a 'keelhauling'?
In some European navies, it was once the practice to tie a delinquent sailor to a yardarm, attach a weight to his feet, and then by means of a rope, 'haul' him through the water from one side of the ship to the other under the 'keel'. The result was often fatal.

Keep mum
Does 'keeping mum' have anything to do with mothers?
No. 'Mum' here is connected to the German for mumble – *mummeln*. It has been used to mean 'keep quiet' for centuries. One of the earliest examples of its use is in the dice game mumchance, which was played in complete silence.

Keep your shirt on
Why do we say to an agitated person, 'keep your shirt on'?
This phrase dates from a time before mass production, when items of clothing were very expensive. If someone got into a fight it made good economic sense to undress first. Telling someone to keep their shirt on was suggesting that it would be much better for them to calm down and avoid the fight altogether.

Kettle of fish

How did we come to call a muddled situation a 'pretty kettle of fish'?
A very popular picnic in Scotland is the 'kettle of fish', so called because the picnickers catch salmon or trout in the streams of the countryside and cook them in a large 'kettle' for the main course. We have a similar phrase – 'pretty picnic' – with a similar meaning. Since 'picnics' are seldom 'pretty' and often do not operate smoothly, both these terms mean the opposite of what they say.

Kick against the pricks

Where did the expression 'kick against the pricks' come from?
Advising someone not to kick against the pricks means don't harm yourself by fighting the inevitable. In Biblical times tillers of the soil used a wooden shaft with a pointed spike, or 'prick', to control the oxen. Sometimes an ox would rebel and kick out at the prick, but as a result it would be driven deeper into the animal's flesh; the more the animal rebelled, the more it suffered.

Kick over the traces

Are the 'traces' that are kicked over marks in the ground?
No. 'Traces' here are the leather straps that connect the collar of a draught horse to the plough or other vehicle. A horse with a leg trapped in the traces might kick out dangerously in an attempt to release itself. The expression is used in a general context to mean behaving without restraint.

Kid

Why do we call a child a 'kid'?
The Anglo-Saxon word for 'child' is *cild*. In ancient times – just as today – people often failed to pronounce the letter 'l'. The similarity of sound between this name for a child and that for a young goat, and the similarity of their antics, led to the use of 'kid' as a synonym for 'child'.

Kilkenny cats

Why do we say two bitter opponents 'fight like Kilkenny cats'?
Because of the Irish legend of two cats that fought until only their tails remained. This legend is supposed to refer to an equally destructive contest between the towns of Kilkenny and Irishtown.

Killed by inches

How did we come to adopt the phrase 'killed by inches'?
The allusion is to the various ways of prolonging death by torture. Procrustes' bed stretched men to death; the iron coffin of Lissa had a lid that was lowered slowly but surely down inside the coffin until ultimately it crushed its victim.

Killed by kindness

Where do we get the expression 'killed by kindness'?

From the story of Draco, the Athenian legislator, who died because of his popularity. The Greeks used to wave their caps and cloaks as a sign of approval and when they were extremely enthusiastic they tossed their hats and their clothing at the object of their enthusiasm. In the sixth century BC, Draco aroused the enthusiasm of the audience in the theatre of Aegina to such an extent, that the entire gathering showered him with caps and cloaks – and smothered him to death.

Kindergarten

How did the 'kindergarten' get that name?

The German word *kindergarten* literally means 'children's garden'. The term was originated by the German educator Friedrich Froebel, who introduced the idea that a school for young children should gratify and cultivate the child's normal aptitude for exercise, play, imitation and construction – just as playing in a garden would do.

Kiss of death

What is a 'kiss of death'?

It's an act or connection with something or someone that is guaranteed to bring ruin. The allusion is to the treacherous kiss Judas gave Christ that led to Christ's immediate arrest, trial and execution.

Kith and kin

What is the difference between 'kith' and 'kin'?

There is little distinction and both terms are almost obsolete except for 'next of kin' for someone's nearest relative. Strictly speaking, though, 'kith' are people one knows and 'kin' are relatives.

Kiting a cheque

Why do we say a person who writes a cheque for more than he has in his account is 'kiting a cheque'?

The term alludes to kite flying – for if you fly a kite, you can never tell definitely when it will return to earth. So too, if you 'kite a cheque' you're never quite certain it won't be presented for collection before you have sufficient funds in the bank. The practice originated as an exchange of cheques between two banks or business firms. Each gave the other a cheque; each deposited the other's cheque in his bank account – and so for a short while each apparently had a larger balance than was actually the case. For many years this was considered a perfectly ethical business practice among banks, businesses and well-established individuals.

Kitty
How did the common pool of a poker game come to be called the 'kitty'?
The term comes from the Middle English word *kist* – from which we also get our modern word 'chest'. A *kist* was a money box – and so, quite logically, the word was applied to the pool of money in a poker game. From being called the 'kist', it became the 'kit', and finally the 'kitty'.

Knickers
Why are knee-length golfing trousers called 'knickers'?
In Dutch, *knickerbacker* is the name of a man who bakes clay marbles. Washington Irvine chose a variant of this name, 'Knickerbocker', as his pseudonym when writing his *History of New York*. Cruikshank's illustrations for this book showed the citizens of New York wearing loose pantaloons caught in at the knee – and so the garments were called 'knickerbockers' or 'knickers'.

Knocked for six
When we're extremely disappointed, why are we 'knocked for six'?
A 'six' in cricket is a ball that is hit over the boundary without touching the ground. The batsman automatically scores six without having to make any runs. Clearly, this would please the batsman, but the saying actually applies to the bowler, who would be feeling less than happy about having delivered the ball that made the high score possible.

Know the ropes
Why do we say someone who knows what's going on 'knows the ropes'?
The phrase comes from sailing: an experienced sailor will 'know the ropes' aboard ship.

Knuckle under
What is the reason we say someone who gives in 'knuckles under'?
Originally, a 'knuckle' was any joint – we still occasionally say 'knuckle of veal' – and in this expression the 'knuckle' referred to is the knee. When you 'knuckle under' you kneel in submission.

Kowtow
Where does the word 'kowtow' come from?
The word is Chinese and literally means 'knock the head'. It was an ancient Chinese custom to touch the ground with the forehead when worshipping or paying one's respects to an illustrious personage. These days, when someone kowtows they respectfully do the accepted thing.

Lackadaisical

Why do we say a lazy, dawdling person is 'lackadaisical'?

It's a bit of keen psychological observation. The term comes from the exclamation, 'lackaday', which means 'shame on you, day' – just as though the 'day' were a person. Since most persons who cry 'lackaday' and blame the quick passage of time are looking for an excuse for their own lack of energy, they are 'lackadaisical'.

Laconic

Where does the word 'laconic' for concise come from?

From 'Laconia' – the general name for Spartan territory. The Spartans were noted for their brusque speech – the best example of it being their reply when Philip of Macedonia wrote to their magistrates: 'If I enter Laconia I will level Lacedaemon to the ground.' The Spartans' reply was: 'If.'

Landlubber

How did the 'landlubber' get that name?

The 'lubber' is not, as so many suppose, from 'lover', but from the Danish *lobbes*, meaning a 'clown' or 'bumpkin'. So the term means any person who lives on land and is inexperienced or awkward aboard a ship.

Larceny

Where did the word 'larceny' get the meaning 'theft'?

In France – where mercenary troops were generally expected to indulge in petty theft. The French word for a mercenary soldier is *larcin*.

Lavender

Why was the flower known as 'lavender' given that name?

It was once the custom – unfortunately, no longer followed – for a laundress to place a sprig of this plant in with the laundry she had cleaned in order to scent it. The Italian word for laundry is *lavanda*.

Lay an egg

How did the expression 'lay an egg' become associated with a joke that falls flat?

A hen that lays an egg makes a great fuss over it, but the other hens pay little or no attention to her. In a similar way, when a comedian tells a joke and makes a great fuss about it but no one else does, then he too is said to have laid an egg.

Lead balloon

What does it mean when something 'goes down like a lead balloon'?

That it wasn't received as enthusiastically as had been hoped. A balloon should go up, but a lead balloon would descend immediately and with a heavy thud.

Leap year

Why is leap year so called?

Normally, as one year follows another, the day of the month that falls on, for example, a Monday this year will fall on a Tuesday next year; and on a Wednesday the following year. In the fourth year it will – after February – 'leap over' Thursday and fall on a Friday.

Learn by heart

Why do we say we learn things 'by heart' rather than 'by head'?

It's because of a mistaken analysis of anatomical functions made by the ancient Greeks. They placed the seat of thought in the heart.

Learn by rote

Why do we use the phrase 'learn by rote' to indicate learning by repetition?

This phrase means 'to learn by the wheel' – from *rota*, the Latin word for wheel. The allusion is to turning the thought over and over in the mind or saying it over and over again – just as a wheel goes round and round.

Leatherneck

Where did the US Marines get their nickname 'leathernecks'?

Sailors gave them that name – from the fact that in 1805 a stout leather collar was sewn on the Marines' coats to ward off enemy sword strokes.

Leave no stone unturned

When we search for something as thoroughly as possible, why do we 'leave no stone unturned'?

This comes from the Greek myth of King Eurystheus, who set Hercules the twelve labours. Eurystheus wanted to kill Hercules' sons after his death and demanded that no stone be left unturned in the efforts to find them. Euripedes included the phrase in one of his plays.

Left the building
How did this phrase come to mean that an event has ended?
An announcement used to be made at the end of Elvis Presley concerts ('Elvis has left the building') to encourage his fans to go home. More recently it was used as the final words of the theme song from *Frasier*, the hit American TV series.

Left holding the baby
How did this come to mean being left on your own to deal with a tricky situation?
The expression was originally applied to a woman made pregnant but abandoned by her lover in order to avoid his parental responsibilities. A variation, 'left holding the bag', meant to distract somebody who would unwittingly stay to take the blame while the perpetrators slipped away from the scene of a crime.

Left in the lurch
Where did we get the expression 'left in the lurch'?
Lurch is a game that is similar to backgammon. The game is marked by inserting pegs in two rows of holes in a board, one after the other, as the player makes a fresh score. Once up and down the board completes a game. If one player has gone up and down the board before the other has finished going up, he wins what is called a 'lurch' or double game – and the opponent is left far behind 'in the lurch'. 'Left in the lurch' now means left in a vulnerable position.

Legend
Why do we call a fable a 'legend'?
The word comes from the Latin *legenda*, which in turn comes from *legere*, meaning 'to read'. The original 'Legenda' was a book describing the lives of the saints that was read at convents and monasteries. It included so much that was far-fetched and miraculous that the word 'legend' got its current meaning.

Leopard
How did the 'leopard' get its name?
Because of a mistake. It was once wrongly believed that the leopard was a cross between a 'leo' (that is, a lion) and a 'pard' (that is, a white panther) – hence the name 'leopard'.

Let the cat out of the bag
Why has a person who has divulged a secret 'let the cat out of the bag'?
It was once the custom for farmers to bring a suckling pig to market in a bag. Sometimes, however, a farmer would substitute a cat for the pig. If the townsman was foolish enough to buy this 'pig in a poke' without first looking inside, he was cheated out of his money. But if someone 'let the cat out of the bag' the deceit was uncovered.

Let her rip

Why do we use the expression 'let her rip' to mean let everything happen as it will?

The 'rip' is a callous punning on RIP (*requiescat in pace*), the Latin inscription on gravestones. This phrase means 'rest in peace'. When we 'let her rip' we allow 'her' to do just the opposite.

Lewd

How did the world 'lewd' acquire its present meaning?

This is an old Anglo-Saxon word *loewed*, meaning 'lay' – as opposed to the clergy. Thus it originally meant 'people generally'. But since at one time only the clergy were able to read or write, 'lewd' was used to mean 'the unlearned'. From 'unlearned' it came to mean 'base' – and ultimately 'vulgar' – language and behaviour', especially in a sexual sense.

Lick and a promise

Why is a quick wash a 'lick and a promise'?

This is probably a fanciful reference to the way a cat licks its paw and passes it over its face as if promising it will have a proper wash later.

Lick into shape

What is the origin of the expression 'lick into shape'?

It was once believed that bear cubs were shapeless at birth and that they remained that way until the mother bear awoke from her long winter's hibernation and literally 'licked them into shape'.

Life of Reilly

Where did we get the expression 'living the life of Reilly'?

This expression had its origin in a comic song of the 1880s about a saloon keeper in a small town in the Middle West, who prospered so much that he was able to raise his saloon to the dignity of a hotel. The song was called 'Is That Mr Reilly?' and was sung by the original Pat Rooney. The chorus goes:

> Is that Mr Reilly, can anyone tell?
> Is that Mr Reilly who owns the hotel?
> Well, if that's Mr Reilly they speak of so highly,
> Upon my soul, Reilly, you're doing quite well.

Lily-livered

Why do we say a coward is 'lily-livered'?

Because the ancient Greeks believed that the liver was the seat of passion. Dark bile indicated strong passion; light bile, weakness. The person whose bile was lily-coloured or white just had no 'guts' at all.

Limbo
What is the origin of the term 'limbo'?
In theology many an infant who has died cannot go to Heaven because of being unbaptised: but neither can the baby go to Hell – because he or she hasn't sinned. The child must therefore stand on the dividing line between the two – and the Latin word *limbus* means 'the edge'.

Limelight
Why do we say that a person of prominence is in the 'limelight'?
Because at one time, calcium – or 'lime' – was an element in making the light of a spotlight. In order to produce a brilliant white light, a stream of oxygen and another of hydrogen were burned upon a ball of lime.

Limey
How did the British sailor get the nickname 'limey'?
This name for a sailor in the British Navy goes back to 1795 – when lime juice was issued by the Admiralty to prevent scurvy. The sailors were first called 'lime-juicers' and then 'limeys'.

Lion's share
Why is the major portion of something called the 'lion's share'?
The allusion is to one of Aesop's fables – in which the 'lion's share' is all. In this fable the lion went hunting with the fox and the ass. As they were about to divide the game, the lion spoke up and demanded one third as the share agreed upon and one third by virtue of his sovereignty. 'And as for the remaining portion,' said the lion, 'I defy anyone to take it from me.' From 'totality', it has come to mean the majority.

Lip service
What is paying 'lip service'?
It's saying you agree with something when really you don't – in other words you're lying. It's a Biblical expression from the book of *Isaiah*: 'This people… with their lips do honour me, but have removed their heart far from me.'

Lobbying
Where do we get the expression 'lobbying'?
Men who wished to promote special interests were at one time allowed the use of the legislative chambers. Because of their insidious persistence, however, they were ultimately banished to the 'lobby' of the chambers – where they seemed to do just about as well!

Lock, stock and barrel
How did 'lock, stock and barrel' come to mean 'all'?
There are three parts to a gun – the barrel, the stock and the firing mechanism, or lock. By saying all three, the speaker means 'everything'.

Lollypop
Why is a 'lollypop' so called?
In northern England the word 'lolly' means 'tongue'. A sweet or lump of candy that you 'pop' in and out of your mouth on to your tongue is quite aptly called a 'lollypop'.

Long run
Why do we use 'in the long run' to mean the final outcome?
The reference is to a race – best illustrated in the Aesop tale of the hare who was ahead in the early stages of the race but lost out to the tortoise 'in the long run'.

Longshoreman
What is the 'long' doing in the word 'longshoreman'?
In the past when ships were unloaded, the sailors passed the goods across from the ships to men who stood 'along' the shore – and so they were called ''long-shore-men'.

Loony
Is there any relationship to the loon implied in the term 'loony'?
Yes. Though the loon is not a crazy bird, its weird, loud cry sounds like the laugher of an insane person. However, the choice of the word was no doubt influenced by its similarity in sound to 'lunacy'.

Loophole
What was the original 'loophole'?
The narrow window in a fortification through which an arrow could be fired with very little danger to the archer. We use it now, especially in a legal context, to mean a tiny means of escape from a difficult situation.

Loose cannon
Why is a 'loose cannon' so dangerous?
The cannons in old sailing ships were massive and heavy and one that came loose from its fastenings could do immense damage to the ship and crew as it rolled with the vessel. It has come to mean someone who is dangerously unpredictable and destructive.

Lord of Misrule
Who is the 'Lord of Misrule'?
The term is not a synonym for the devil. The 'Lord of Misrule' was originally the 'Abbot of Misrule' – the person designated as 'Master of Revels', somewhat like the 'king' of a Mardi Gras.

Lost the plot
What does it mean when you've 'lost the plot'?
This modern expression is used when you don't know what's going on or have forgotten your objective. It derives from losing track of the plot of a book, play, film or television programme.

Lotus eater

How did a person who fritters away time get the name 'lotus eater'?

Homer's *Odyssey* tells of those who, because they ate the fruit of the lotus tree, forgot their friends and homes and lost all desire to return.

Love

Why do we use the word 'love' to mean 'zero' in tennis?

The term comes from the French *l'oeuf*, meaning 'egg'. The French use it to designate 'no score' or 'zero' because an egg looks like an '0'. When the game was imported into England from France the term was also introduced, but its spelling was changed to 'love'.

Low road

What are the 'high road' and the 'low road' in the song 'Loch Lomond'?

The 'high road' is the highway, of course; but the term 'low road' refers to an old Celtic belief that, when a man meets his death in a foreign land, his spirit returns to the place of his birth by an underground fairy way – by the 'low road'. The song tells of two wounded Scottish soldiers, held prisoner in Carlisle jail. One of them was to be released; he would take the high road home to Scotland. The other was to be executed; he would take the low road. But the dead man, travelling by the low road with the speed of a spirit, would naturally – or supernaturally – be in Scotland before the living, who would have to tramp the many weary miles of the high road before he could hope to reach Scotland. It is this thought which consoles the Scot singing as he is about to die.

Luck of the Irish

Why do we call a surprising turn of good luck the 'luck of the Irish'?

Because although they have suffered episodes of extreme poverty and hardship, the Irish have always managed to pull through somehow. The 'luck of the Irish' has saved them time and time again.

Lumber

What is the origin of the word 'lumber'?

Since the first pawnbrokers came from the Lombardi region of Italy, their shops were called 'Lombard shops'. Pawnbrokers generally have a great many odds and ends lying about their shops taking up space – and so any space-filling miscellany was called 'Lombard'. In time the word became 'lumber'. Because the sawed timber, barrel staves and ship masts left lying around in the dealer's yard take up a lot of room, the yard was called a 'lumber yard'. From this the timber itself came to be called 'lumber'.

Lump it

How did the word 'lump' get into the expression 'if you don't like it you can lump it'?

A person's face will often look swollen and lumpy after crying. So to 'lump it' is to sulk or look sulky – and the phrase 'like it or lump it' means 'like it or sulk'.

Lush

Why do we call a drunkard a 'lush'?

The City of Lushington was the name of a convivial society made up chiefly of actors that met at the Harp Tavern in London until about 1895. The society had a 'Lord Mayor' and four 'aldermen' – from 'wards' named 'Jupiper', 'Poverty', 'Lunacy' and 'Suicide'. It was the duty of the 'Lord Mayor' to lecture new members on the evils of drink. A member of this society was known as a 'lush' but by a process of reversal the word came to be applied to a drunkard.

Lynch law

What is the origin of the term 'lynch law'?

Charles Lynch was a Justice of the Peace of Bedford County, Virginia, in 1780 when gangs of Loyalists were ravaging the countryside – more like robbers than men fighting for a cause. Many of these men were captured, but at that time the only court in Virginia authorised to try felonies was in Williamsburg, and Lynch discovered that the Loyalists sent there for trial were being rescued before they arrived. So they set up a rump court of their own to try their prisoners. Lynch and his associates kept strictly to legal forms in these trials and put down much of the prevailing lawlessness; however, the setting up of the court itself was unlawful. The courts imposed heavy fines and corporal punishment was often inflicted – but the only person to be hanged was a slave convicted of poisoning his master's wife. Nevertheless, today a 'lynching' is almost always a hanging without any trial at all.

Macaroni

Why, in the song, did Yankee Doodle call himself 'macaroni'?

Because it was once a name for a fop or dandy. A group of well-travelled young Englishmen of wealth and position formed a club called the 'Macaroni Club' in London around 1760. They chose this name because of their fondness for foreign cooking. These young men also dressed in a foreign manner; the common people misunderstood the use of the word 'macaroni' and took the name of their club to be descriptive of their dress.

Machiavellian

How did the word 'machiavellian' come to mean 'evil scheming'?

Niccolo Machiavelli of Florence wrote a book called *The Prince*. It expounded the art of government and showed how, by treachery and other despicable acts, it was possible for a prince to achieve and uphold arbitrary power.

Mad as a hatter

Why were hatters prone to madness?

Because of the mercury heated and used in treating the felt for the millinery trade. Mercury vapour affects the nerves, causing uncontrollable twitching or, at worst, serious brain damage.

Mad as a March hare

Why do we say 'mad as a March hare'?

March begins the mating season for hares and the rutting hares run about wildly at that time – apparently quite mad.

Magazine

Why is a periodical called a 'magazine'?

Because it's considered to be a storehouse for numerous articles. The term comes from *makhzan*, the Arabic word for 'storehouse', and was originally applied to a place used by the Army for storing arms. The word 'magazine' was first used in its present sense in 1731 when *The Gentleman's Magazine* was first published.

Magenta
Why is the colour 'magenta' called that?
It comes from the Battle of Magenta of 1859. The colour was developed shortly afterwards and was named to commemorate the battle.

Make the bed
Why do we say we 'make' the bed when we spread the sheets and blankets?
We speak of 'making' the bed, instead of tidying it, because beds were once created anew each night from straw thrown on the floor.

Make the grade
Does 'make the grade' refer to academic grading?
No. 'Grade' here is short for 'gradient'. The expression derives from railroad construction in nineteenth-century America. The massive task of linking the east and west coasts, required careful calculations to ensure the route avoided any gradients that the engines would not be able to surmount – or 'make'. 'Making the grade' means reaching the required standard.

Make no bones
How did the expression 'make no bones about it' come to mean frank speech?
The early meaning of this expression, now almost forgotten, was 'to let things pass'; a guest finding a bone in his or her fish soup or chowder would, for politeness' sake, 'make no (mention of the) bones'. Then the phrase began to be used in a satirical sense to mean just the opposite.

Make one's mark
Why do we say a person who has achieved success has 'made his mark' in the world?
At one time smiths and other artisans made distinctive marks on their wares so it could be identified as their own. If the artisan's mark became generally known, he had 'made his mark' in the world. The idea of a person 'making his mark' – that is, placing his name – on the pages of history is of later origin.

Man flu
What is 'man flu'?
Almost certainly nothing more than a common cold, but the suffering male will declare that he has influenza and will take to his bed. The expression was no doubt coined by an exasperated woman, who had soldiered on when afflicted with exactly the same virus as her partner.

Manna
Where did 'manna' get that name?
From the Israelites who first saw this 'food' spread upon the ground. From the Biblical description of manna we can deduce that it was hail; but the Israelites did not know what it was – and so they exclaimed '*Man-hu*' – which, translated literally, means 'what is it?'.

Mansard roof
What is the origin of the 'mansard roof'?
Paris in the eleventh century limited the number of floors to a building.
The French architect Francois Mansard, got around this law by lifting up
one of the slopes of the roof, making it higher than the other, and creating,
in effect, an extra storey.

Mantelpiece
How did the 'mantelpiece' get its name?
From the fact that it was once just a shelf over a fireplace on which coats,
cloaks and 'mantles' were hung to dry.

Many a slip
Why do we say that there's 'many a slip 'twixt the cup and the lip'?
The expression is an allusion to the legend of the Greek slave of Ankaios,
who had been helmsman of the Argo. The slave told his master that he
would never taste the wine that came from his own vineyard. He was
right. Just as Ankaios was ready to lift the cup to his lip and drink, he heard
that a wild boar was wreaking havoc in his vineyard. Ankaios rushed out
and the boar killed him.

Mardi Gras
Where did 'Mardi Gras' get that name?
The term is French and literally means 'Fat Tuesday'. It got its name from
the French custom of parading a fat ox as part of the celebrations of
Shrove Tuesday, the last day before the start of Lent.

Married at the church door
What is the origin of the expression 'married at the church door'?
The phrase was once literally true. Some five hundred years ago it was
the custom in England to perform the wedding ceremony at the door of
the church. After it was over, the couple entered the church for Mass. Later,
the ceremony was moved inside for communicants of the church; only
when one of the parties to a Catholic marriage was Protestant, or divorced,
or otherwise 'undesirable', was the ceremony performed at the door.

Martinet
Where did the 'martinet' get that name?
From a commander of the French infantry. In the reign of Louis XIV of
France, General Martinet remodelled the French infantry by instituting
very strict discipline based upon severe punishment – so severe that the
French call a cat-o'-nine-tails a 'martinet'. The English adopted the term
as a synonym for a strict disciplinarian.

Maudlin

Why is an over-sentimental person said to be 'maudlin'?

The term is an impious reference to Mary Magdalene – a British pronunciation of Magdalene being 'maudlin', as in Magdalene College, Cambridge. Medieval painters represented Mary Magdalene as having a very doleful face, her eyes swollen with weeping.

Maverick

Why is a wayward, rebellious person called a 'maverick'?

In Texas around 1840, one Samuel Maverick began raising cattle. Maverick failed to brand any of his calves – which led to wholesale rustling of Maverick stock. From this any unbranded animal found roaming came to be called a 'maverick'.

Mealy-mouthed

Why do we say a sweet-speaking person is 'mealy-mouthed'?

Because 'mealy-mouthed' is just an improper pronunciation of the Greek *melimuthos*; *meli* means 'honey', while *muthos* means 'speech'.

Melancholy

How did we get the word 'melancholy'?

The term comes from the Greek *melaina*, meaning 'black' and *chole*, meaning 'bile'. The early Greeks thought that the emotions were made active by bile – and that a sorrowful feeling was created by black bile.

Mend fences

What do we do when we 'mend fences'?

We take action to resolve a dispute. It originated from the old proverb 'good fences make good neighbours', meaning that it's a lot easier to get on with someone you are, of necessity, in very close proximity to if the boundaries are clearly defined.

Mentor

Why is a mental or moral guide called a 'mentor'?

Mentor was the name of a faithful friend of Odysseus, whose form the Greek goddess of wisdom Athene assumed when she accompanied Telemachus in his search for his father. So the term means a wise counsellor and guide.

Method in one's madness

What is the meaning of 'method in one's madness'?

That there is an element of sense in what may appear to be inexplicable behaviour. The source is *Hamlet*: 'Though this be madness, yet there is method in't.'

Midas touch

Why do we say a lucky person has the 'Midas touch'?

This comes from one of the most famous Greek myths. King Midas, offered a gift by the god Dionysius, greedily chose to have everything he touched turn to gold. Unfortunately, he was unable to eat or drink gold, and he even turned his beloved daughter to gold when he embraced her. He was able to undo the spell by immersing himself in the River Pactolus. Nowadays we have forgotten the negative connotations and now say someone who can make a success of anything has the 'Midas touch'.

Milliner

What is the origin of the word 'milliner' for a hat designer and maker?

At one time the city of Milan set the fashion throughout the world – much as Paris did at a later date. The 'Milaner' was, therefore, a stylist – and from this came 'milliner'.

Minister

How did a 'minister' come to be called that?

The word literally means an 'inferior person' or 'servant'. The original idea was that a minister was supposed to serve his parishioners, a notion that has not yet completely disappeared.

Minutes of a meeting

Why are the notes of a meeting called 'minutes'?

Because these notes are generally made in 'minute' or small writing – that is, in shorthand.

Miscreant

Where do we get the word 'miscreant' from for a wrongdoer?

The term is from the French *mescreant* and literally means an 'unbeliever'. It was first applied by the Christians to the Mohammedans – who in turn called the Christians 'infidels' – since neither side believed the other followed the 'true' religion.

Mollycoddle

How did a weak person come to be called a 'mollycoddle'?

'Molly' is a familiar pet form of 'Mary', which was once contemptuously applied to a wench or prostitute and later to a gangster's 'moll'. This use led people to call an effeminate man a 'Molly' – and to 'mollycoddle' yourself is to take far too much care of yourself.

Monkey jacket

Why do we call a mess jacket a 'monkey jacket'?

No reference to the organ grinder's monkey is intended. A 'monkey jacket' is one without tails – and so should more properly be termed an 'ape jacket'. The name was first applied to the short jacket worn by sailors.

Monkey wrench
Where did the 'monkey wrench' get that name?
According to tradition, this wrench with a movable jaw adjustable by a screw was first made by a London blacksmith named Charles Moncke. The tool was originally called a 'Moncke wrench' – just as a 'Stillson wrench' today bears the name of its inventor. But since few people knew the true origin of the word, it was soon corrupted into 'monkey wrench'.

More than one string to his bow
Where does the expression 'more than one string to his bow' come from?
From England. British archers long followed the prudent practice of carrying a spare bowstring when they went to war. A man who had 'more than one string to his bow' was certainly well prepared.

Moron
What is the origin of the word 'moron'?
The word is pure Greek, but was arbitrarily given to adults with a mental age of eight to twelve years by Dr Henry H. Goddard in the early twentieth century. Classifying the mentality of sub-normal people into three groups; those with the lowest intellect would quite obviously be called 'idiots' and the middle group 'imbeciles' – but the highest group needed a new name. So Dr Goddard picked out of his Greek lexicon the word *moron*, meaning 'dull, stupid, silly, foolish' – all of which he felt to be an accurate description of this group.

Mosey
How did 'mosey' come to mean a slow walk?
The term comes from the Spanish *vamose*, meaning 'let's go'. We've preserved the word in its entirety to indicate rapid travel – in the form of 'vamoose' – and we use the last syllable to mean slow travel.

Mother Earth
Why do we speak of the Earth as 'great Mother Earth'?
Among almost all peoples, the Earth has at one time been reverenced as the 'mother' of all. The Romans, for instance, tell the story of how the two sons of Tarquinius, together with Junius Brutus, asked the Delphic Oracle which one of them would succeed to the throne of Rome. The oracle replied, 'He who shall first kiss his mother'. The two sons of Tarquinius raced home to find their mother, but Junius Brutus fell to the ground saying, 'Thus I kiss thee, oh Earth, great mother of us all'. He became King.

Moveable feast
What is the meaning of a 'moveable feast'?

A 'moveable feast' in general usage is an event that has no fixed date or time. The term is ecclesiastical; moveable feasts are those that are linked to Easter, the date of which is fixed each year by lunar rather than calendar timing. When used in relation to feasts, 'moveable' is spelled with an 'e' before the 'a'.

Mud in your eye
How did 'here's mud in your eye' come to be an accepted toast?

The expression is not a toast to another; it is a toast to yourself – for it means 'I hope I beat you'. The allusion is to a horse race. If the track is at all muddy, the rider of a losing horse is very likely to get mud-splattered eyes from the horse in front.

Mufti
Where did we get the word 'mufti' to describe casual clothes?

Indirectly from Arabic. A Mohammedan priest is called a *mufti* and his clothes aren't at all like ours. In the early nineteenth century, English music hall comedians represented the Army officer off duty as wearing a dressing gown, smoking cap and slippers – and since this dress was not the usual garb of an officer they called him a 'mufti'. The officers themselves picked up the term and started to call their leisure clothes mufti.

Mug
Why do we use the word 'mug' to mean our face?

Because a comparatively small jug used for drinking is called a 'mug' and in the eighteenth century in England they were commonly shaped and decorated to resemble a human face.

Muscle
Where did we get the word 'muscle'?

From the Latin *musculus*, which means 'little mouse'. If you tense and untense the muscles of your upper arm, you will see what looks like a little mouse crawling back and forth under your skin.

Nail one's colours to the mast
Where does the expression to 'nail one's colours to the mast' come from?
From naval warfare. In a battle at sea a ship surrenders by striking its colours – that is, lowering its flag. If the colours are 'nailed to the mast' they cannot be lowered and the ship cannot surrender; it must fight on no matter what happens. We say this to denote a firm commitment to a particular course of action.

Naked truth
Why do we call absolute truth the 'naked truth'?
Because, according to ancient legend, Truth and Falsehood once went bathing. When they came out of the water, Falsehood ran ahead, dressed herself in Truth's clothing and sped away. Truth, unwilling to appear in Falsehood's clothing, went naked.

Navel gazing
Why do we say someone immersed in their own thoughts is 'navel gazing'?
This refers to the practice of Eastern mystics, who aid their passage to a trance by staring fixedly at their own navels. The Greeks even have a word for this form of meditation: *omphaloskepsis*.

Neat as a new pin
Why does 'neat as a new pin' mean extremely tidy?
In the days before pins were made of brass or were coated with tin, they were made of iron wire and rusted quickly. Only a new pin of this type was without blemish.

Nemesis
Why do we call something that pursues you relentlessly your 'nemesis'?
In Greek mythology, Nemesis was an avenging goddess who saw to it that people were punished for their misdeeds. The literal translation of *nemesis* is 'remorse'.

Nest egg
How did something put by for an emergency get the name 'nest egg'?
It was once a common practice, when collecting eggs from a hen roost, to leave behind a single egg in each nest – so that the hen would continue to lay. From this, 'nest egg' got the meaning of something laid by to take care of the future. It's interesting to note that this practice, though no longer necessary with domestic fowl, is still effective with other birds. Once a bird starts to lay, it will usually continue laying long enough to put the normal number of eggs for that species in the nest. An experiment on one songbird, in which each day all but one egg was removed from the nest, led to the production of 72 eggs – though the usual clutch was fewer than six.

Never darken my door
Does 'never darken my door' come from Victorian melodrama?
No. It was used much earlier in 1729 by Benjamin Franklin when writing under the pseudonym 'Busy Body': 'I am afraid she would resent it so as never to darken my doors again.' However, we do more commonly think of a command from a stern Victorian father while throwing an errant son or daughter out of the family home. 'Darken' here refers to casting one's shadow across the threshold of the house.

Nick of time
How did we get the expression 'in the nick of time'?
In medieval days, a tally was used to register attendance in colleges and churches. The tally was a stick of wood, and attendance was indicated by a nick or notch cut on it. The student or worshipper who arrived in time had his attendance 'nicked' – and so arrived 'in the nick of time'.

Nine days' wonder
Where did the phrase 'nine days' wonder' come from?
This expression originally referred to the novena of the Roman Catholic Church – and 'novena' comes from the Latin *novenas*, meaning 'nine each'. The patron saint of each church is accorded a novena, which lasts for nine days – during which time the image of the saint, relics and other sacred objects are paraded for the 'wonder' or veneration of the worshippers.

Nineteen to the dozen
Why do we say something very fast is going 'nineteen to the dozen'?
This expression came from Cornish tin and copper mines in the eighteenth century. Pumps were installed to drain flooded mines and when working at full capacity, they could clear nineteen thousand gallons of water for every twelve bushels of the coal that powered them. This was a vast improvement on the hand pumps that had been used previously.

Niobe's tears
What is the origin of the term 'Niobe's tears'?
The name for perpetual weeping comes from Greek mythology. Niobe, Queen of Thebes, was the mother of seven sons and seven daughters. When the people of Thebes gathered for their annual celebration of the feast of the goddess Latona, Niobe appeared and told them to worship her instead – for she was queen and had seven times as many children as Latona. They obeyed. Latona became indignant and asked her children, Apollo and Diana, to help restore her prestige in the eyes of the people. Angered at the slight to their mother, they flew to the city of Thebes and slew all 14 of Niobe's children. In spite of her grief, the Queen continued to berate Latona; thereupon she was changed to stone – yet Niobe's tears continued to flow. She was finally borne upon a wind to her native mountain where she still remains – a mass of rock from which a trickling stream flows, product of her never-ending grief.

Nip in the bud
Does 'nip in the bud' derive from horticulture?
Yes. Unwanted growth can be prevented by nipping off buds or shoots as soon as they appear. We use this expression to mean destroying or slowing growth before it gets out of control.

No great shakes
How did we come to say something of little importance is 'no great shakes'?
The term comes from shooting dice. If you shake and throw a losing number, it is certainly 'no great shakes'.

No quarter
Why do we say we give 'no quarter' when we mean we show no mercy?
Because originally to 'give quarter' meant to send conquered enemy soldiers to a special section or 'quarter', where they remained until their fate was determined. They could be set free, ransomed or enslaved. If they were killed instead they were given 'no quarter'.

No such thing as a free lunch
Is there really 'no such thing as a free lunch'?
Not according to economic theory, which says that whatever is provided must be paid for by someone. The concept of the 'free lunch' was well known in America and Britain – but it did not refer to charity. It was the free food provided by saloon and inn keepers to entice customers into the premises. Doubtless the profit on the accompanying liquid refreshment more than compensated for the expense of the food.

Nod is as good as a wink
Why do we say 'a nod is as good as a wink'?
The original phrase was 'a nod is as good as a wink to a blind horse'. In other words, there's no point in nodding or winking at a person who can't see you. But we have changed the meaning of the expression to indicate the ability to take a hint – and so, of necessity, have dropped all reference to the horse.

Nodding acquaintance
Why is someone you know only slightly a 'nodding acquaintance'?
This dates from the days of complicated rules of etiquette. If you met someone in the street to whom you had already been introduced, you might greet them with a bow or curtsey and conversation could correctly follow. However, if the connection was only very slight, the proper form of recognition was a brief nod of the head and then passing on.

Nose to the grindstone
How did we come to say a busy man 'keeps his nose to the grindstone'?
A man who is very busy literally and figuratively 'humps himself' – he bends over. This brings his nose forward; and if he's busy grinding, it makes him appear to be grinding his own nose.

Nostrum
Why do we call a quack medicine a 'nostrum'?
Nostrum is a Latin word meaning 'of us' or 'ours'. The quacks of the Middle Ages – who used puppets and acrobats to attract crowds and help them sell their medicines – refused to divulge their contents or formula, saying 'it's ours' – '*nostrum*'.

Not cricket
Why is something unfair 'not cricket'?
Cricket is usually considered a sportsmanlike game played by gentlemen, so unfair play or cheating is simply 'not cricket'.

Not over till the fat lady sings
Where did we get the expression 'it's not over till the fat lady sings'?
It could have originated from sport (also, 'the fight/game ain't over till the bell rings') or from bored churchgoers ('church ain't out till the fat lady sings'). Or, since 'the opera ain't over till the fat lady sings' is the most often heard variant, its true foundation may lie in the fact that so many operas end with a full-on aria delivered by a well-built soprano. However, the saying certainly stems from America and may even be a Southern proverb. It is used to remind people who believe an outcome is certain that it's the final result that matters – sometimes in a spirit of reassurance, but also sometimes as a warning against over-optimism.

Not a sausage
Why does 'not a sausage' mean broke?
It's Cockney rhyming slang: sausage – sausage and mash – cash. To have 'not a sausage' means you have no cash.

Not worth a rap
Why is something that's practically worthless 'not worth a rap'?
Because there was a great scarcity of small coins in Ireland in the 1700s and so a counterfeit halfpenny that was introduced gained wide circulation. This coin was called a 'rap' – and it was worth no more than a quarter of its face value.

Nuts in May
Where is the sense in the expression 'here we go gathering nuts in May'?
No 'nuts' at all – the original word was 'knots'. In other words, sprigs of flowers that bloom in May.

Off the wall

Does 'off the wall' refer to a snooker shot off the side of the table?

It may do, though there is another possible snooker-related source. A player might prefer to use his or her own cue rather than selecting a potentially inferior one from the wall-mounted racks in the room. So if a person's behaviour is 'off the wall', it is as crazy and unpredictable as a shot from a bent snooker cue.

Off your own bat

Is 'off your own bat' related to cricket?

Yes. A score made by a batsman's own hits is made solely by his own efforts, and that is how we use the phrase generally – when someone succeeds by only his own endeavours.

Okay

Where did we get the expression 'okay'?

From the US Presidential election of 1840. The Democratic candidate, Martin Van Buren, was nicknamed 'The Wizard of Kinderhook' – after 'Old Kinderhook', the Hudson Valley village in which he had been born. In reference to this village and Van Buren's nickname, one of the Democratic groups formed to support him in New York City called itself 'The Democratic OK Club'. Other supporters of Van Buren in New York picked up the term 'OK' or 'okay' as a sort of slogan, and Democratic rowdies used it as their war cry in their attempts to break up Whig meetings. The phrase caught on generally and soon established itself as synonymous with the feeling of the original club members – that they and their candidates were 'all right'.

Old boy network

What is the 'old boy network' used to get on in life?

It is the favouritism network that exists between people who went to the same school, most often a public school such as Eton or Harrow. By exploiting the 'old boy network', one might achieve advancement rather than through one's own merits or experience.

Olive branch
How did 'extending the olive branch' come to be an offer of peace?
The olive branch is a very ancient symbol of peace. It appears in Greek mythology in this context. In the Bible the return to Noah's Ark of the dove bearing an olive leaf was a sign that the flood created by God in anger was over.

On the back burner
Why is something that can be left alone for a while to return to later 'on the back burner'?
The back burner of a stove tends to be smaller and less powerful, so food can be left to cook without needing any attention. This 1950s expression therefore means no harm will come from leaving something metaphorically 'simmering' until the time is right to go back to it.

On the cards
Does 'on the cards' derive from gambling?
No. The cards referred to are the Tarot pack used in fortune telling. When something is 'on the cards' it is very likely to happen.

On the carpet
How did 'on the carpet' come to mean a reprimand?
Originally, only the boss's office had a carpet. So, to be called 'on the carpet' was to be called into the boss's office – and this usually meant a telling off.

On the level
Where did we get the expression 'on the level'?
The term originated in Freemasonry. The level is an emblem of that organisation – as is the square – and the Masons first used 'on the level' as well as 'on the square' to describe someone, especially other Masons, as being utterly reliable.

On the stocks
Are the 'stocks' in this saying the ones used for public punishment?
No. It is a reference to the wooden framework on which a ship was supported while under construction. Something 'on the stocks' is in the process of being prepared.

On tick
How did we come to call charging a purchase buying 'on tick'?
In the seventeenth century, 'ticket' was the standard term for a 'due bill' or written acknowledgement of a debt. 'On tick', therefore, means 'on the ticket' – that is, by promissory note rather than by cash.

On the wagon
What is the origin of the expression 'on the wagon'?
The term comes from the Army, where wagons carrying water once accompanied troops on the march. After a heavy night of drinking and carousing, a man was often in need of copious drinks of water – as well as inclined to swear off liquor for good. For this reason the man, literally as well as figuratively, climbed on the water wagon.

Once in a blue moon
Why do we use the expression 'once in a blue moon' to mean very rarely?
Because the phrase originally meant 'never' – and a blue moon was supposed never to occur. But moons of blue colour have been seen after certain volcanic explosions and occasionally through smoke-laden fogs – and for this reason perhaps the phrase now means 'hardly ever'. The expression is also used to describe a second full moon in a calendar month, which occurs once every two or three years.

Ordeal
Where does the word 'ordeal' come from?
From the Old English word *adaelan*, meaning 'to deal out'. From this idea of giving to each his or her share, 'ordeal' came to mean 'judgement'. It was once the custom to try a man by subjecting him to torture – in the belief that God would protect and defend the right, even by a miracle. This form of judgement by torture was called an 'ordeal' – whence the present meaning of the word.

Ostracise
Why do we say a person who's kept out of a group is 'ostracised'?
The word comes from the Greek *ostrakon*, meaning a 'tile'. It was the custom in ancient Greece to send into exile for five or ten years a person whose power or influence was considered dangerous to the state. This decree of banishment was effected by taking a vote on the question – and the voting was done with tiles on which the person's name was written.

Ouija board
How did the ouija board get that name?
'Ouija' is a compound of the French *oui* and the German *ja* and no doubt is derived from the fact that the ouija board agrees with its operators; it is a mechanical 'yes man'.

Out of the frying pan into the fire
What do we mean by 'out of the frying pan into the fire'?
That we are going from one bad situation to another. The expression is self-explanatory, but most languages have an equivalent phrase. The Greeks say 'out of the smoke into the flame'; the Italians 'fall from the frying pan into the coals'; and the Gaelic version is 'out of the cauldron into the fire'.

Ovation
Where did we get the word 'ovation' for triumphant acclaim?
From the Romans. But the Roman 'ovation' was only a second-class celebration for a lesser triumph – a battle won without bloodshed, or a victory over slaves. The honoured citizen did not appear in a chariot but only on a horse or on foot.

Over a barrel
Why do we say we have someone 'over a barrel' when we can get them to do anything we want?
An early form of inquisition involved holding someone over a barrel of boiling oil. The alternatives for the victim were either to agree to the demands or be dropped in the barrel; in other words, they had no choice at all. Being able to 'wrap someone round your little finger' means very much the same thing.

Over-egg the pudding
Why do we say we 'over-egg the pudding' when we spoil something by not knowing when to stop?
A pudding or cake with the right quantity of egg will be light and delicious. But adding more egg will not make it even better: on the contrary, it will be soggy and unrisen.

Over the moon
Were footballers the first to call being ecstatically happy 'over the moon'?
No, although it's been a cliché only since the 1970s when football adopted the phrase. It was originally a slang expression used by 'The Souls', a group of arty Victorians and Edwardian aristocrats. They took it from the nursery rhyme in which 'The cow jumped over the moon'.

Paddle your own canoe

Where does the expression 'paddle your own canoe' come from?

The phrase was first used in a poem published in *Harper's Magazine* for May 1854:

Leave to Heaven, in humble trust,
All you will do to
But if you would succeed, you must
Paddle your own canoe.

When you paddle your own canoe, you will succeed at your task entirely by your own efforts.

Pagan

How did a pagan get that name?

The Christian church made its converts first in the cities, next in the villages, and lastly in the country. 'Pagan' is from the Latin *pagus* and literally means 'belonging to a village'.

Pain

What is the origin of the word 'pain'?

This word literally means 'punishment'. It's from the Latin *poena*, meaning penalty. The original idea must have been that anyone who suffers pain must deserve punishment – for Adam's sins, if not for his or her own.

Palace

Where did we get the word 'palace'?

From Rome – for the word originally meant a dwelling on the Palatine Hill in Rome. The Emperor Augustus built a home there – and so did Tiberius and Nero.

Pall Mall

How did 'Pall Mall' get its name; and why is it pronounced 'pell mell'?

In the Italian ball game called *palamaglio*, the players run about in apparent reckless confusion. When this game was introduced to England, it was called 'pall-mall' – from the Italian *palla* meaning 'ball' and *maglio* meaning 'mallet'. Though the English spelled the name 'Pall Mall', when they named the playing ground – and later the street and park – after the game, they pronounced it 'Pell Mell' from their 'pell-mell' manner of playing it. 'Pell-mell' itself is from the French *pêsle-mêsle* – the *pêsle* being just rhyming duplication for emphasis of *mêsle*, meaning 'mix'.

Pallbearer

Why is a person who carries a coffin called a 'pallbearer'?

The Romans called the square piece of cloth they threw over their shoulders a *pallium* – and so any sort of covering is a 'pall'. Pallbearers once carried the coffin under a pall – though today this covering is not widely used except in military funerals.

Palm it off

Why is getting rid of something by passing it on to another called 'palming it off'?

The expression comes from card playing. If a cardsharp, about to deal a card to himself, discovers (by peeking) that it's one he doesn't like he may hide it in the palm of his hand and deal himself another. Then he will 'palm off' the bad card to one of the other players.

Pan out

Where did we get the expression 'pan out'?

It's a gold-mining term. One method of obtaining gold dust is to take a handful or so of the sand in which it's found and place it with a little water in a shallow pan. Then, by sloshing the water back and forth, the lighter sand, dirt and pebbles can be sluiced over the edge while the gold dust, which is heavier, will remain – and so 'pan out'. When everything 'pans out', it all resolves satisfactorily.

Panic

Why do we call sudden widespread fear 'panic'?

Sounds heard on the mountain tops and in the deep valleys at night were once attributed to the Greek god Pan. He was believed to be the cause of any sudden, groundless fear – and so such a fear was called 'panic'.

Paper tiger

Where does the expression 'paper tiger' come from?

China. It was used by the Chinese Communist leader Mao Tse-Tung in 1946 as a term of abuse directed at America. A 'paper tiger' may look formidable, but is in fact highly fragile.

Paraphernalia
How did personal belongings come to be called paraphernalia?
According to Roman law there were certain things that a wife might claim as hers upon the death of her husband – articles that weren't a part of her dowry. The Romans adopted a Greek word to cover these items, *parapherna*, meaning 'beside dower'.

Pariah
Why do we call a social outcast a 'pariah'?
Because the 'pariah' of India belongs to one of the lowest castes of Hindu society. He gets his name from the Timbal word for 'drummer', *paraiyan* – because he plays the drums at Hindu festivals.

Parlour
How did the parlour get its name?
'Parlour' comes from the French *parler*, meaning 'to speak' – it's really a 'conversation room' in which you entertain your guests. ('Drawing room' is short for 'withdrawing room' – the room to which you withdraw after a meal.)

Parthian shot
Why do we use the term 'Parthian shot' to indicate a final thrust as one departs?
Because that's how the Parthians fought. They used to charge on horseback at their enemies, shooting arrows at them. But then, instead of stopping to fight, they'd ride away again – shooting arrows till out of range.

Pass the buck
What is the origin of the expression 'pass the buck'?
In an old English card game a jacknife – or 'buck' – was passed from player to player to show whose turn it was to chip in. The procedure was adopted in poker and a buck was passed from player to player to indicate whose turn it was to deal – and, as dealer, add a chip to the pot. Since only the dealer could stack or juggle the cards, 'passing the buck' came to mean passing on responsibility for an honest deal.

Pay the piper
Why do we use the phrase 'pay the piper' to indicate future remorse?
Because, though dancing is fun, the piper who leads or plays for the dance must be paid. The moral is pointed out in the story of the Pied Piper of Hamlin, who wasn't paid for ridding the town of rats and so led the town children away for ever.

Pea jacket
How did the 'pea jacket' that sailors wear get that name?
The term is derived from the Dutch *pije*, meaning 'coarse thick cloth or felt' – and refers to the cloth used in making the pea jackets. The sailor's jacket that is sometimes called a 'reefer', is so called because it is close-fitting and pulled in tight – like a sail that has been reefed.

Pear-shaped

Why do we say something that has gone badly wrong has gone 'pear-shaped'?

The true derivation of this saying, which appeared in the 1960s, is not known. One interesting theory is that it is RAF slang for an in-flight acrobatic such as a loop-the-loop that doesn't quite come off – instead of a perfect circle, the pilot makes a pear shape.

Pecking order

Is the expression 'pecking order' related to birds?

Yes. A pecking order is the hierarchy of poultry. The most powerful bird pecks a bird of lower status, who in turn pecks another of an even lower rank, and so on. Inevitably, the most inferior bird in the flock, with no other left to peck, is at the bottom of the pecking order. The same system operates in human society, especially in the workplace: the most superior and most inferior of a community is determined, and also where all the rest fit in between.

Pedagogue

Where does the word 'pedagogue' come from?

From the Romans. In ancient Rome, a pedagogue was a slave who took the children to school, to the theatre and on their outings, and often taught them as well. The word comes from the Greek *paed*, meaning 'child', and *agein*, meaning 'to lead'.

Peeping Tom

Why do we call a person who makes a practice of sneaking a look a 'Peeping Tom'?

It's because the tailor who tried to get a look at Lady Godiva as she rode naked through the streets of Coventry – in a protest against the taxes imposed upon the people – was named Tom. This particular 'Peeping Tom' was struck blind.

Penny has dropped

Where does the expression 'the penny has dropped' come from?

Almost certainly from the penny-in-the-slot machines that used to be on piers and arcades. They do nothing whatsoever until the penny has dropped in the mechanism, and then they spring to life. If a person initially fails to understand a joke he will look blank: once he gets it – when 'the penny has dropped' – you will be able to tell from his reaction.

Petticoat

Why is a woman's underskirt called a 'petticoat'?

Originally the garment was a 'petty coat' – a small coat worn by men under their coat of mail or doublet. Then women adopted the garment – they too wore a short or 'petty' coat. But in time they lengthened the garment and lowered its support until it reached from the waist to below their knees.

Philanderer
Why is an inconstant lover said to be a 'philanderer'?
The word literally means 'loving man'. It's from the Greek *philos*, meaning 'loving' and *andros*, meaning 'man'. Somehow it became linked to a person, often a man, who was unable to stay faithful.

Philippic
Why do we call a verbal attack a 'philippic'?
Demosthenes attempted to arouse the Athenians to resistance against Philip of Macedonia. His orations against 'Philip' are 'Philippics' – hence this name for a strong speech in which one person attacks another.

Philosopher
How did the philosopher come to be called that?
The Greek word for 'wise' is *sophos* – and the sages of Greece were once called that. But Pythagoras thought this word too arrogant and so added the word *philos*, meaning 'loving'. The *philos-sophos*, or 'philosopher', is therefore a 'lover of wisdom'.

Phoney
Where did we get the word 'phoney' as a synonym for 'false'?
From an American manufacturer of cheap jewellery named Forney. Forney specialised in brass rings that looked like gold. He sold these rings by the barrelful to street peddlers and soon the rings came to be known by them as 'Forney rings'. The pronunciation and spelling was in time changed to 'phoney' and the word was extended to apply to other forms of jewellery – and eventually to anything and anyone fake.

Pidgin English
Where did 'pidgin English' get that name?
Pidgin, formerly 'pigeon' is what Chinese traders made of the English word 'business' – 'bidjiness' to 'bidjin' to 'pidgin'. Pidgin languages are a means of communication between people with no common language and are often used in business and trading situations.

Pig iron
How did 'pig iron' come to be called that?
Molten iron from a blast furnace is run into moulds dug in the sand; these moulds are a series of parallel trenches connected by a channel that runs at right angles to them – and the whole looks something like a sow with a litter of suckling pigs.

Pig in a poke

Why do we refer to the risky business of buying something sight unseen as 'buying a pig in a poke'?

A 'poke' is a bag – from the Irish word for it, *poc*. It was once the custom to bring small pigs to market in a bag. If you bought such a 'pig in a poke' without looking at it you didn't really know what you were getting.

Pigeonhole

Why is one chamber of a tier of compartments called a 'pigeonhole'?

Because a dovecote – the home of domesticated pigeons – is usually divided into many little compartments, each one, literally, a 'pigeon hole'.

Pillar to post

How did we come to say a person is tossed 'from pillar to post'?

The expression refers to the fact that at one time an offender against law and order was either placed in the pillory or whipped at the whipping post – and was sometimes forced to go from one to the other. We use it when someone is going backwards and forwards between one difficult situation and another.

Pin money

What is the origin of the term 'pin money'?

When pins were introduced at the beginning of the sixteenth century, they were made of silver and considered quite a luxury. For this reason they were used as gifts on New Year's Day. In time, instead of giving his wife a gift of pins, the husband merely gave her the money to buy the pins. Then the term was extended to signify the sum of money a man gave his wife each year – or upon their marriage – for her private expenses. Finally, 'pin money' became recognised in law and a wife could sue to collect pin money – but only for one year's worth. Nowadays, pin money is what we call a small sum of money a man, woman or child may have that is entirely for him or her to spend.

Pinch of salt

Why do we say a questionable statement should be 'taken with a pinch of salt'?

Because salt added to food brings out the flavour. If you are presented with something and 'swallow it whole', you may not notice any taint – but if you take it 'with a pinch of salt' the salt will accentuate the flavour and enable you to test its worth.

Pipe dream

Why do we say an impossible aspiration is a 'pipe dream'?

The substance being smoked in this context was opium, which produces elaborate fantasies. At one time opium was a legal (and widely used) drug in the form of laudanum.

Plain sailing
Why is an uncomplicated course of action 'plain sailing'?
This phrase was used as early as 1683 in a handbook for apprentice sailors: *A token for ship-boys, or plain-sailing, made more plain*. Nautical plain sailing is progressing on calm, easy-to-navigate waters: generally it means a simple, trouble-free passage to the desired destination.

Play a straight bat
What do we mean when we say someone 'plays a straight bat'?
A cricket batsman will keep his bat as straight and vertical as possible when facing challenging bowling in order to deal with variation in the height of the bounce. In general usage, we say someone plays a straight bat when he or she deals with an unwelcome question by giving a noncommittal or evasive answer.

Platform
What is the reason we call a political party's statement of its aims a 'platform'?
Political candidates must appear before their constituents in order to win their votes. To be seen and heard, they must stand upon a platform. The platform is constructed of planks. From this, the statement of political faith upon which they stand – or fall – is called a 'platform' and its various parts are known as 'planks'.

Pleased as Punch
Why do we say we're as 'pleased as Punch'?
Because in the standard Punch and Judy show, Punch carries a stick with which he batters Judy – and then bursts into screams of laughter.

Plucky
Why do we call a brave man 'plucky'?
The 'pluck' is that which is 'plucked' from the innards of a bird or an animal preparatory to serving it at the table – the heart, gizzard, liver and guts. A 'plucky' man is one who has 'guts' – and we use both terms to mean emotional stamina and stability.

Plus fours
How did golfers' short trousers come to be called 'plus fours'?
Ordinary knickerbockers, or knee-breeches, were not full enough at the knees to allow a full swing in playing golf. So, in making golf knickers, 4 inches were added to the length of the seam to allow the knickers to hang over the knees and thus give the player enough slack. The tailor's notation for this was '+4'.

Poetic justice
What do we mean by 'poetic justice'?
It indicates that the treatment meted out to someone is appropriate to their actions. 'Poetic' here has the enhanced meaning of earlier times – righteous, honourable, moral and sweet.

Point blank
Where did we get the expression 'point blank'?
From the French. The centre of a target was once a small white spot and the French for white is *blanc*. The French *point* means 'aim'. So the term literally means, 'aim at the centre of the target'. 'Point blank range' is a range so short you can hardly miss the target.

Poke bonnet
Why was a 'poke bonnet' called that?
This bonnet got its name from the fact that it poked out at the front far beyond the face: a bonnet that didn't do so was called a 'kiss-me-quick'.

Poker
How did the game of poker get that name?
The game is German in origin and gets its name from the German *pochen*, meaning 'to boast' or 'brag' – though a literal translation is 'to knock'. A 'knock' is still used in poker to indicate a passed bet – and the game still includes considerable 'bragging'. But the game seems to have been introduced into America through New Orleans where, due to its similarity to the French game of *poque*, it acquired that name. Southern gentlemen who played the game but were untutored in French pronunciation gave it two syllables – 'pok-uh' – which sounds very similar to 'poker'. Northerners who learned the game from these gentlemen quite obviously deduced, therefore, that it was spelled the same.

Pope
How did the Pope get that name?
The term comes from the Italian *papa*, meaning, of course, 'father'.

Porcelain
Why is chinaware called 'porcelain'?
The word originates from the French *porcelaine* – and literally means 'like a pig'. The back of cowrie shells look something like a pig's back and so these little shells were named 'little pig' shells. Chinese earthenware has a white glossy look like the inside of these shells – and so it too was given this name.

Port

Why do we call the left side of a vessel the 'port' side?

The steering oar of ancient sailing vessels was on the right, or 'starboard' side. The opposite, or left, side was therefore the one laid up against the dock for unloading. This side was nearest the 'port'; and, if necessary, it had in it a cargo 'port' or opening. Both terms come from the same Latin root *port*, meaning 'opening'. The change from calling this side of the vessel 'larboard' was brought about by the confusion often arising out of the similarity of sound between 'larboard' and 'starboard'.

Porterhouse steak

Who was the Porter for whom the 'porterhouse steak' was named?

He was an early New York tavern keeper. The 'Porter House' was famous for its steaks, but on one occasion ran out of them. So, Porter dipped into the larder and took out a large piece of sirloin he'd been keeping for roasting. He cut a piece and broiled it. The steak was found to be delicious and was added to the bill of fare as 'porterhouse steak'.

Posthaste

Why do we use 'posthaste' to mean as fast as possible?

Because back in the days when all travel was by horse, travelling by post – that is by public coach – was faster than travelling by private carriage. The owner of a private vehicle had to stop to rest his horses, but 'post horses' were used in relays and the coach kept rolling.

Pot calling the kettle black

What do we mean when we say the 'pot is calling the kettle black'?

This expression describes those who accuse others of having faults that they themselves have. It goes back to the days when cooking was done over an open fire, and pots and kettles were likely to be equally blackened by the smoke.

Potluck

What is the reason an impromptu meal is called 'potluck'?

It was once customary for the housewife to have a pot on the fire into which all scraps of meat and vegetables were thrown. She kept the pot boiling and there was always stew available – but what you got and how it tasted was a matter of potluck.

Pound of flesh

Why is something that is owing called a 'pound of flesh'?

The source is Shakespeare's *Merchant of Venice*, the drama of which centres on Shylock's insistence that the hero Antonio repays the pound of his own flesh he wagered in a financial deal. The figurative use of the phrase refers to ruthless, though lawful, pursuit of what is owed.

Pouring oil on troubled waters

Why do we speak of pacifying someone or a situation as 'pouring oil on troubled waters'?

It's a scientific fact that oil poured on a rough sea will lower the waves. The scientist Benjamin Franklin, on hearing this Biblical phrase, decided to test its literal truth. He poured oil on the ocean and found the waves were considerably reduced.

Powwow

Why do we call a council a 'powwow'?

'Powwow' is a Native American word. The Native Americans of the New England coast first used it in referring to their medicine man; then it was transferred to their ceremonial rites; afterwards, it came to mean any gathering at all.

Prestige

What is the origin of the word 'prestige'?

It comes directly from the Latin *praestigium*, meaning a 'delusion' or 'illusion'. The plural of this Latin word, however, means 'jugglers' tricks'. But there is a Latin term that more nearly approximates to our concept of 'prestige' – *praestringere oculos*; this means 'to blindfold' and, by analogy, 'to dazzle the eyes'.

Printer's devil

How did a printer's assistant come to be called a 'printer's devil'?

The apprentice boys of early print shops so often had their faces begrimed with ink that they looked as black as any devil employed to stoke the furnaces of Hell – and so they were called 'devils'. The story is told that when Aldum Manutius, the sixteenth-century Venetian printer, employed a black boy as a helper, the people of the city – who had rarely, if ever, encountered a black person – became convinced the boy was an imp. Accusations were made against Aldus, and in defence he was forced to publish this notice: 'I, Aldus Manutius, printer to the Holy Church and to the Doge, have this day made public exposure of my "devil". All who think that he is not flesh and blood may come and pinch him.'

Private soldier

Why do we call a common soldier a 'private' soldier?

Because at one time in England the men who entered government service in any executive capacity – including those who became officers in the army – were said to have entered 'public life'. Others were called 'private citizens'. The common soldier was a private citizen who enlisted or was drafted into service. Since it was presumed that he had not adopted soldiering as a career, he was called a 'private soldier' as opposed to a 'public officer'. In time, however, 'public' was dropped from in front of the word 'officer' and 'soldier' from after the word 'private'.

Prize ring

How did the square space where two prize fighters meet come to be called a 'ring'?

The reason is to be found in the history of the rules of the sport. Figg, the first recognised boxing champion of England, adopted his own set of rules. These called for a square of 8 feet drawn in the centre of the stage. Within this square the rival fighters 'toed the mark', as it was then termed, or 'squared off' to begin hostilities. Later, Broughton's rules were adopted. They called for a second square, a yard across, to be drawn in the middle of the larger square. 'For every set-to', the rules said, 'the rival seconds must bring their men to opposite sides of the square from where the fighting should begin.' Still later, when the contestants were first made to keep the fight within a square enclosure, the rules said: 'There shall be drawn in that square a circle five feet in diameter, known as the centre, where contestants shall meet for the beginning of each round.' It is this 'ring' that has given its name to the enclosure in which the boxers meet.

Proletariat

Where does the term 'proletariat' come from to describe people of a lower social class?

From the Latin *proletarius* – the name given by the ancient Romans to the lowest class in the community. 'This class', the historians of that time said, 'contributes nothing to the state but offspring.'

Prude

Why do we call a prissy person a 'prude'?

Because the French think of a proud woman as being discreet. The French use the word *prudefemme* – which literally means 'proud woman' – to denote a discreet woman and we have taken our 'prude' from this word – adding the aspect of being overly prim.

Pull one's leg

Why do we say that one person joshing another is 'pulling his leg'?

The allusion is to tripping up someone by catching at their foot or 'pulling their leg'. This, of course, makes one fall – and seeing a person fall is considered comic by all of us … isn't it?

Pull one's weight

Is 'pull one's weight' a sporting metaphor?

Yes, but unusually the sport is rowing. If one crew member fails to row with the energy appropriate to his weight, then the rest of the crew has to make up the difference. To 'pull one's weight' is therefore to do as much as one is capable of.

Pull out all the stops

Why do we 'pull out all the stops' when we put the maximum effort into an activity?

The 'stops' here are the knobs on an organ console that the player pulls in and out to bring different pipes into play. If all the stops are pulled out the instrument makes the maximum noise.

Pull your finger out

Where did the expression 'pull your finger out' come from?

It's an old nautical piece of essential advice. When a cannon was loaded, the small amount of gunpowder needed to set off the charge was held in place by a crew member inserting a finger in the ignition hole. It was obviously wise for him to remove his finger when the cannon was about to be fired. When we tell someone to pull their finger out, we are saying 'get a move on!'.

Pumpernickel

Why is 'pumpernickel' bread called that?

The name of this special type of bread is German. In German 'nickel' is a common abbreviation of the personal name 'Nicolaus', while 'pumper' means 'the noise of a heavy fall'. Somehow the combination of these two words came to mean 'a coarse, dark-complexioned, brutish fellow' – and pumpernickel bread is both coarse and dark.

Pup tent

How did the 'pup tent' get that name?

These small tents were named by the Union soldiers in the American Civil War. When they were introduced and the soldiers told to use them, they appeared so much like dog kennels to the men that one of them stuck his head out and began barking. The idea soon took hold and soon the whole camp was barking. The tents were, therefore, called 'dog tents' – the name soon degenerating into 'pup tents'.

Puppy

Where does the word 'puppy' come from?

From the French *poupée*, meaning 'doll'. By extension, it came to mean any sort of plaything – including a young dog.

Purchase

How did the word 'purchase' get its present meaning?

'Purchase' comes from the French *pourchasser*, which means 'to hunt'. Once upon a time, stores had no windows in which to display their goods and would-be purchasers had to 'hunt' for what they wanted – though they were helped somewhat by apprentices who stood outside the stores and asked what they wanted as they passed by.

Put one's oar in
Why is interfering 'putting one's oar in'?
This derives from an expression that is at least five hundred years old and may be much older. Having 'an oar in every man's boat' is being involved in everyone's affairs. A similar saying is 'having a finger in everyone's pie'.

Put on side
Why do we say a pretentious person 'puts on side'?
A 'side coat' is a long, trailing coat – from the Anglo-Saxon *sid* meaning 'great', 'wide' or 'long'. 'Putting on side' is to dress in a side coat or other long clothing and act the superior person.

Put a sock in it
When was this first said to mean 'shut up'?
In the early twentieth century. In the first days of radio broadcast there was almost no technology to control the volume of musical instruments. Socks were stuffed into the mouths of brass instruments as a makeshift mute. The veteran jazz trumpeter Humphrey Lyttelton has told of how, in the absence of a sock, various items of undergarments were employed to the same end. The implication in general use is that a speaker should put a sock in his or her mouth to stop their talking.

Put through the mill
Why is suffering an ordeal being 'put through the mill'?
The allusion is to grain being crushed by a millstone.

Pyrrhic victory
Why do we call a success gained at too great a cost a 'Pyrrhic victory'?
It is an allusion to the victories of King Pyrrhus of Epirus over the Romans in about 280 BC. With a force of 25,000 men, Pyrrhus met the Romans under the Consul Laevinius at Heraclea – the first time that Greeks and Romans had engaged each other in battle on such a large scale. In the end, because of his cavalry and the accompanying elephants, Pyrrhus severely defeated the Romans – but not until both sides had suffered extremely heavy losses. Rome refused to make peace with the victor and the following year Pyrrhus again defeated the Romans at Asculum – in these two engagements he lost most of his army. According to Plutarch, when Pyrrhus was congratulated on the victory he said, 'Such another victory and we are utterly undone'.

Q

Quack

Why is a medical charlatan called a 'quack'?

Because he boasts of his salves. 'Quack' is really an abbreviation of 'quacksalver', which comes from the Dutch *kwakzalver* – and this has this idea of 'quacking about one's salves'. But the idea behind all these derivations is that the 'quack' is like the duck – and makes a big noise over nothing.

Quaker

How did the Quakers get that name?

George Fox, the founder of the Society of Friends, in his speeches admonished the magistrates of England and told them they should 'quake at the word of the Lord'. The term 'Quakers' comes from this phrase and was coined by Justice Bennet, a magistrate of Derby.

Quarantine

Where does the word 'quarantine' come from?

From the Italian *quaranta*, meaning 'forty'. In early days, a ship suspected of being infected with some contagious disease was kept outside of port for 40 days – in 'quarantine'.

Quibble

Why do we call a petty argument over a minor point 'quibbling'?

The word comes from the Latin *quibus*. This is the dative and the ablative of *qui*, meaning both 'who' and 'which' – and it was used so much in legal documents and fought over to such an extent by lawyers that it gave us the term 'quibble'.

Quinsy

How did the illness 'quinsy' get that name?

The word comes from the Greek *kynanche*. This means both 'sore throat' and 'dog collar' – because a dog collar produces a choking effect. People suffering from acute quinsy often find it difficult to open their mouths and so have a feeling of choking.

Quintessence

Why do we call the ultimate essence the 'quintessence'?

Because the ancient Greeks believed there were four forms in which matter could exist – fire, air, water and earth. But the Pythagorean philosophers added a fifth form – ether. It was more subtle than the others and was considered the purest. This was the fifth essence; the Latin word *quintus* means 'fifth'.

Quiz

How did 'quiz' come into the English language?

Because of a bet. A man named Daly, who was manager of the Dublin Theatre, made a bet that he would introduce into the English language within 24 hours a new word that had no meaning. Accordingly, on every wall and accessible place in Dublin, Daly chalked up the four mysterious letters Q–U–I–Z. That day all Dublin was inquiring what they meant, the people saying to each other: 'Quiz? Quiz? What does it mean?' Daly won his bet – and the word has remained in our language to this day. It is quite probable, however, that his choice of letters – or at least, the continued popularity of the term – was influenced by the similarity in sound and meaning to the word 'inquisition'.

Rabbit punch
Why do we call a punch behind the ear in boxing a 'rabbit punch'?
Because at one time a poacher catching a rabbit in a snare, which in itself had not killed the animal, would finish it off with a sharp blow on the back of the neck.

Rack one's brains
Why is a person who is struggling to remember something said to 'rack his brains'?
As used here, 'rack' means 'to stretch or strain by force' – as a tortured person was stretched on the rack or wheel – and that is a rather vivid metaphorical description of the process of remembering.

Radar
How did 'radar' get its name?
It's just a combination of the initial letters of 'radio direction and ranging' – an exact description of what it does.

Radio
Where did 'radio' get that name?
The word is derived from the Latin *radius*, meaning a staff or the spoke of a wheel or a ray of light. Radio waves travel like rays of light – going out in all directions like the spokes of a wheel.

Ragtime
How did we come to call syncopated music 'ragtime'?
The term 'ragtime' originally meant haphazard, careless and happy-go-lucky. It was applied to an army under loose discipline – as opposed to one that was made to keep step. Ragtime music is equally happy-go-lucky and careless of the music as written.

Rain check
What does 'I'll take a rain check' mean?
That the speaker wishes to defer an event or invitation, as a sporting event might be postponed because of bad weather. It is mainly used as a kinder way of declining an invitation than a blunt 'no'.

Rain on my parade
What do we mean by 'don't rain on my parade'?
Obviously, a street parade would be ruined by a rainstorm – think of the soggy paper decorations, sodden participants and miserable spectators huddled under umbrellas. So we say this when someone tries to dampen our enthusiasm for a forthcoming happy occasion. A distinctly vulgar variation is 'don't piss in my bucket'.

Raining cats and dogs
What is the origin of the expression 'raining cats and dogs'?
It comes from Norse mythology – in which the cat symbolises heavy rain, while the dog, an attendant of Odin, the storm god, represents great blasts of wind. The proverbial enmity of cats and dogs must have led to the choice of these animals to represent the conflict of the elements in a storm.

Raising Cain
Why is causing trouble 'raising Cain'?
According to both the Bible and the Qur'an, Cain, the son of Adam and Eve, was the first murderer. If you bring about disorder, you might as well be the unhappy parents of Cain.

Rank and file
Who are the 'rank and file'?
Those who form the majority of any group or organisation, other than the leaders. The phrase is military in origin; enlisted men marched in ranks (close abreast) and files (one behind another), while officers marched outside the formation.

Raspberry
Why do we 'blow a raspberry' to express contempt?
It comes from Cockney rhyming slang: raspberry – raspberry tart – fart.

Rat race
Why do we call the frantic pace of modern life the 'rat race'?
The comparison is with laboratory rats, futilely running around a maze or in a wheel trying to escape.

Read between the lines
What do we do when we 'read between the lines'?
We are finding additional meaning from a statement or situation that has not actually been stated. The expression refers to the practice of writing secret messages in invisible ink 'between the lines' of ordinary writing.

Real estate
Where did land get the name 'real estate'?
From England – where the term originally meant a 'royal grant'. All land once belonged to the king in England, and the only way a person could own any of it was by royal grant.

Real McCoy
Why do we use the phrase the 'real McCoy' to mean genuine?
A prize fighter by the name of McCoy was being annoyed by a drunk. The pest wanted McCoy to fight but, being a professional boxer and realising the man's condition, McCoy refused. Friends tried to calm down the drunk by telling him that he was hassling the famous fighter McCoy; the drunk didn't believe them and finally became so annoying that McCoy punched him and knocked him out. When he came to, the drunk said: 'You're right; he's the real McCoy.'

Red herring
How did we come to call misdirection 'drawing a red herring across the trail'?
This term for an attempt to distract attention from the main issue comes from fox hunting. Because of the way it's cured, a red herring has a very strong odour. Hounds set on the scent of a fox may be distracted by the smell of a red herring dragged across the trail and then follow the trail of the red herring instead of that of the fox.

Red-letter day
Why do we call an important day in our lives a 'red-letter day'?
In the early prayer books, the Saints' days and church festivals were printed in red ink. Some prayer books are still printed in this style and many calendars today have the Sundays and holidays indicated by red letters or figures. So, a 'red-letter day', since it's a holiday, is one that we look forward to or back on with pleasure.

Red tape
Where did governmental delay get the name 'red tape'?
From Britain, where for centuries its government has followed the custom of tying up official papers and document cases with red tape. The everlasting tying and untying of the tape led to its choice as an illustration of useless delay. The present British 'red tape' is pink.

Rhyme or reason
Why do we say something nonsensical is 'without rhyme or reason'?
Some poems have no sense to them but at least have 'rhyme'; some prose is awkward but at least has 'reason'. Something that has neither is no more than rubbish.

Right foot foremost
Where did we get the expression 'right foot foremost'?
From ancient Rome – where it was once believed that bad luck was brought to a house by a person who crossed the threshold with his left foot. This belief was so strong that a servant was often stationed at the door, to make sure all visitors entered the house 'right foot foremost'.

Right and left

Why do we refer to a conservative political party as a 'party of the right' and a liberal party as a 'party of the left'?

Because that's how they are traditionally seated in the legislatures of European countries. The presiding officer was generally a man of position and therefore a conservative. So he seated the conservatives on his right, to honour them more than the liberals he seated on his left.

Right off the reel

How did we come to say a person with ready answers gives them 'right off the reel'?

The original meaning of this phrase was 'without intermission' rather than 'without hesitation', and the allusion is to a rope or thread being unwound – off the reel.

Ring the bell

Why do we say a success 'rings the bell'?

You don't find them as often as you would have in Victorian times, but county fairs may feature a strength-testing machine that is operated by hitting a block with a sledgehammer. This activates a wooden arm that sends a weight up a wire. If you hit the block hard enough, the weight will go to the top of the device and ring a bell. The usual prize for this achievement in the heyday of this test-your-strength machine was a cigar. Similarly, if you hit the bull's eye at a shooting gallery you ring a bell.

Ring the changes

Why do we 'ring the changes' when we alter the way we usually do something?

The reference is to bell ringing. Traditional bell ringing does not produce a tune; instead the bells are sounded according to various mathematical formulas. When the bell ringers 'change', they play a succession of peals.

Ringleader

Why is the leader of a group of people called a 'ringleader'?

The term comes from dancing. Many old dances began with all the participants holding hands in a ring. Then the circle was broken and one person led the rest of the 'ring' through the figures of the dance.

Rise

Why do we say we 'get a rise' out of a person when he shows he can't take a joke?

The expression comes from angling. If you place the right lure in the right spot at the right time, the fish will 'rise' to the bait – and be caught.

Rival

What is the derivation of the word 'rival'?

It comes from the Latin word for 'stream' – *rivus*. The original rivals were people who lived on opposite sides of a stream and fought bitterly over which side of the stream was the better to live on.

Rob Peter to pay Paul
Where did we get the expression 'rob Peter to pay Paul'?
Originally from the supposed rivalry between St Peter, who was the Apostle to the Jews, and St Paul, who was the Apostle to the Gentiles. But the expression has undoubtedly survived because of the alliteration.

Rocket science
What do we mean when we say something is 'hardly rocket science'?
That it's such a simple concept, it's unbelievable that someone can't grasp it. This usage does lead one to wonder what actual aeronautic and astronautic specialists say when their colleagues are slow off the mark – when what they do is, literally, rocket science.

Rope them in
Why do we say a successful attraction 'ropes them in'?
The term is an allusion to the once common practice of drawing in hay with a rope. After the cut hay had been heaped in rows (windrows), a rope with a horse at each end was swept like a net around the row, bringing the hay together into a stack.

Rotten apple
What is a 'rotten apple'?
A bad person who will have a negative effect on any people he or she comes into contact with – in the same way that one rotten apple in a storage barrel will contaminate all the rest.

Rough diamond
Who might we describe as a 'rough diamond'?
A rough diamond (also a 'diamond in the rough') is someone who is basically good-hearted but lacking in social graces – and possibly operating only just on the right side of the law. The phrase is a metaphor for diamond gemstones, which, though unpolished and coarse when newly mined, have all the potential to become brilliant jewels.

Round the bend
Where did the expression 'round the bend' to mean 'mad' come from?
Victorian mental hospitals were frequently situated in grand houses. A bend was put in the entrance drive so the premises was not mistaken for a stately home, which would usually have a straight drive.

Round robin
Why is a petition signed by a number of people called a 'round robin'?
It's because such petitions were originally signed in a circle so that no single person could potentially be identified as the instigator heading the list. The term is a corruption of the French *rond*, meaning 'round', and *ruban*, meaning 'ribbon' – the circle of signatures creating the impression of a 'round ribbon'.

Royal road to learning
Where did we get the expression 'the royal road to learning'?
From the legend of 2,200 years ago, that the King of Egypt asked Euclid if there wasn't an easy way for him to learn geometry. To this Euclid replied: 'Sire, there is no royal road to learning.'

Rule of thumb
How did rough measurements come to be called 'rule of thumb'?
Because that's one way to make approximate measurements. The first joint of the thumb is approximately one inch long. A 'foot' was once the length of a foot; a 'hand' was the width of a hand; an 'ell', the length of the arm from elbow to wrist; and a 'fathom', the length of the arms outstretched. We still sometimes use a 'finger' to measure drinks.

Run amuck
Where did we get the phrase 'run amuck', meaning 'go wild'?
From Malaysia. Malays under the influence of opium or a stimulant sometimes became very excited – so excited that they rushed about with daggers, killing anyone they chanced to meet and yelling *'Amoq! Amoq!'* – meaning 'kill! kill!'.

Run the gauntlet
What is the origin of the expression 'run the gauntlet'?
A common punishment for a disgraced sailor was to run between two rows of his companions, who had been armed with gauntlets and rope ends. As he ran, every man he passed would deal him as many blows as he could. This was also a custom among North American Indians. We use the expression when someone is persecuted on all sides.

Run of the mill
Why do we say something ordinary, basic or undecorated is 'run of the mill'?
A 'run' in manufacturing jargon is the operation of a piece of machinery from start to finish. Something 'run of the mill' has been through the manufacturing process at a cotton or woollen mill, for example, but is awaiting inspection to determine its quality.

Runcible spoon
How did the 'runcible spoon' get that name?
A 'runcible spoon' is a tined spoon with a sharp cutting edge – in effect a combination of a knife, fork and spoon all in one. It was named in jocose allusion to the Battle of Roncevaux Pass in 778, which was more slaughter than battle.

Sabotage

Where does the word 'sabotage' come from?

The word – which originally meant a wilful destruction of machinery by workmen in industrial disputes – is French and is derived from *sabot*, the name of the French workmen's wooden shoe. When looms were first introduced in France, the workmen of the mills objected to them and threw their clogs into the looms in order to put them out of action.

Sack

How did the expression 'get the sack' come to mean 'discharged'?

In the days when most artisans and mechanics lived on the job, they brought their own tools to work with them in a 'sack'; and then left the tools and sack with their employer for safekeeping. When the mechanic was discharged his employer gave him back his sack of tools – he literally 'got the sack'.

Sail close to the wind

Why do we say following a course that is only just legal is 'sailing close to the wind'?

Because a sailing vessel 'sailing close to the wind' is in danger of being caught by a gust and jibbing or keeling over – and so being swamped. So too, a person engaging in a practice that is just short of being illegal is in danger of being caught.

Salad days

Why is a man's youth his 'salad days'?

It's because when you are young, you're 'green' or immature – and 'greens' go into making a salad.

Salary

Where did we get the word 'salary'?

From the ancient Romans. The word literally means 'salt money'. The Roman soldier was once given an allowance of salt; later he was given an allowance of money for the purchase of salt. This was called a *salarium* – from *sal*, meaning 'salt'.

Sands are running out

Why do we say 'the sands are running out' when we mean that time is getting short?

Because at one time a sand–clock was used to tell the passing of time. It was composed of two glass compartments and the sand trickled from the upper one to the lower. When the top section was almost empty you knew that time was almost up.

Sandwich

Who named the sandwich?

John Montague, the mid-eighteenth-century Fourth Earl of Sandwich loved to play cards so much that he never wanted to take time out to eat. So he solved the problem by placing slices of beef between two pieces of bread and munching away while he played.

Santa Claus

How did Santa Claus get his name?

The term comes from the Dutch dialect name for St Nicholas – *Sint Klass*. St Nicholas is the patron saint of children, and in Holland gifts were once given to children in his name on his feast day of 6 December. In time this custom was transferred to Christmas and it was expanded to include giving gifts to all. St Nicholas is also the patron saint of scholars, travellers, sailors and pawnbrokers.

Sarcophagus

Where do we get the word 'sarcophagus'?

'Sarcophagus' was originally the name of the stone chosen by the ancients for their coffins – and not the name of the coffins themselves. The stone was believed to consume the body placed within it and the name comes from this belief, being a combination of the Greek *sarx*, meaning 'flesh', and *phagein*, meaning 'to eat'.

Sardonic laughter

How did mocking laughter come to be called 'sardonic'?

It's because *Herba Sardonia* – which grows in Sardinia – is a poison so bitter to the taste that it makes the nerves around the mouth go into spasm, causing a painful fixed grin.

Saved by the bell

Why are we 'saved by the bell' when rescued by a last-minute intervention?

'Saved by the bell' is boxing slang. A fighter in danger of losing can be saved from imminent defeat by the bell that is rung at the end of the round. An alternative source stems from the terror people had in the seventeenth century of being buried alive; a coffin was invented that had an internal bell, to be rung if the unfortunate occupant revived – though there is no evidence that these caskets were ever used.

Scapegoat

Why is a person who suffers for another's misdeeds called a 'scapegoat'?

The Book of Leviticus tells how on the Day of Atonement the sins of the people were symbolically placed upon the head of a goat, which was then allowed to escape into the wilderness. Thus the term 'scapegoat' literally means 'escaping goat'.

Schmooze

What is the derivation of 'schmooze' for socialising to make advantageous connections?

It comes from the Yiddish *schumsen* – a combination of 'chat' and 'rumour'. Schmoozing appears to be an acceptable business practice, the idea being that both sides may well benefit from the contact.

School

What is the origin of the word 'school'?

The word is from the Greek and originally meant 'leisure'. In ancient Greece only a person with leisure time could go to school.

Scoop

Where did newspapermen get the word 'scoop' for an exclusive story?

The use of this term comes from poker. If there's a big pot and you are the winner, you 'scoop' up the chips. From this we get the meaning of 'winning over others in large measure' – which is what a paper does when it has a scoop.

Scot-free

Does the 'scot' of 'scot-free' come from Scotland?

No. It comes from the Anglo-Saxon *sceot*, meaning 'money put into a general fund' – hence, a tax. The 'scot' was the original income tax, since it was levied upon the people according to their ability to pay. 'Scot-free' first meant 'tax free'.

Scraping the bottom of the barrel

What are we doing when we are 'scraping the bottom of the barrel'?

We are using the very last and least desirable option, every other available alternative having been tried to no effect. The philosopher Cicero used this metaphor, inspired by the sediment left by wine in a barrel.

Seat of the pants

What does 'fly by the seat of the pants' mean?

Early aeroplanes had limited flight control systems and devices. Pilots flew by feel, responding to what was needed particularly via the largest point of contact between them and the plane – the seat of their pants. The term is generally used when someone works out what to do about a situation as it unfolds.

Send to Coventry
What is the origin of the expression 'send to Coventry'?
During the years of strife between the kings of England and Parliament, small parties of the king's men who visited the dives of Birmingham were frequently attacked and either killed or 'sent to Coventry' – then strongly Protestant and pro-Parliament. In Coventry, of course, the Royalists were ostracised, so no one talked to them.

Seventh heaven
Why do we say we're in 'seventh heaven' when we're as happy as we can be?
Because Muslims believe there are seven heavens piled one upon the other and that each heaven represents greater happiness than the previous one. God himself and the angels are all in the seventh or topmost heaven.

Shanghai
Why do we use the word 'shanghai' to mean kidnapping a man for a ship's crew?
It's because British sailors so treated were likely to find themselves shipped out on a long voyage to a distant port – and since Shanghai was on the other side of the world they used the name of this port to represent any distant place.

Shanty
How did 'shanty' come to mean a tumbledown house?
It started in Canada; *chantier* was the name the early French settlers gave to the hut in the forest that served as their headquarters. Here they slept and stored their tools. 'Shanty' is a corruption of *chantier*.

Shebang
Where did we get the expression 'the whole shebang'?
It comes from an Irish name for a speakeasy – that is, a drinking place without a licence – *shebeen*. A truculent drunken Irishman might try to take on everyone present – 'the whole shebeen'.

Sheriff
How did a 'sheriff' get that name?
The term is derived from the Anglo-Saxon title *shire reeve*. The shire reeve of eleventh-century England was an official who was appointed by the king to administer the local government, enforce the law, and collect the king's taxes.

Shillelagh
Why do the Irish call a truncheon a 'shillelagh'?
The true Irish 'shillelagh' is a truncheon made of oak – and is named for the town of Shillelagh in County Wicklow, Ireland, which is celebrated for its fine oak trees.

Shilly-shally

Why is a person who can't make up his mind 'shilly-shallying'?

The person who can't make up his mind constantly asks himself questions; and the term is a corruption of 'Shill I? Shall I?' – 'shill' being a weak form of 'shall'.

Shimmy

Why do we call a wiggly dance a 'shimmy'?

The dance got its name from an article of clothing – the 'chemise'. When you dance the 'shimmy' you wiggle your hips and shoulders as you would when getting into a chemise. *Chemise* is the French word for 'shirt'.

Shindig

How did a party come to be called a 'shindig'?

If the party gets rough enough, the men begin to fight and 'dig' each other in the 'shins' with the toe of their boot. 'Shindig' was first used in reference to this blow; then to the party itself – though only a rough one – and finally to any party at all.

Ship has sailed

What do we mean by 'that ship has sailed'?

That however unhappy you are about something, there's nothing you can do about it if it's already happened. Its use in this context is fairly recent, and it's encouraging to know that the sea, for centuries the source of countless sayings and expressions, is still generating them today.

Shirt off one's back

Why do we say a really generous person will 'give you the shirt off his back'?

Because this once represented the ultimate in generosity. In the days when men wore only three pieces of wearing apparel – coat, trousers and shirt – a person could give you his coat and still remain fully covered. But if he then gave you 'the shirt off his back', that was all he could give – within the limits of decency.

Shoddy

How did poor quality material come to be called 'shoddy'?

In the process of weaving cloth, a certain amount of fluff is thrown off. This was called 'shoddy', from the dialect verb *shode*, meaning 'shedding' or 'separating'. The fluff was then used in making new wool – but, because the fibres were short, clothes made from it did not last long.

Shoestring

Why do we say that someone who has built up a business from next to nothing, 'started on a shoestring'?

The allusion is to a street peddler who offers shoestrings for sale. This form of business venture requires no office, no tools and less capital than almost any other type imaginable.

Show a leg

Why do we say 'show a leg' when we want someone to wake up and get out of bed?

In the days when sailors were not allowed shore leave, probably for fear they would desert, their 'wives' were sometimes permitted to come on board overnight. In the morning the bosun's mates would give the order to 'show a leg'. If it was a male leg, its owner had to get up and begin work; if female, the lady was allowed to lie in a bit longer.

Shrimp

Is there a connection between 'shrimp' as a nickname for a small person and the seafood?

There is none. The 'shrimp' that is applied to a small person is a corruption of the Anglo-Saxon *scrine-an*, meaning 'to shrink'; it's used humorously to indicate the idea that the person is so small he must have shrunk.

Siamese twins

Why are conjoined twins often called 'Siamese twins'?

The first of these twins to be widely exhibited – Chang and Eng Bunker – were born in Siam (now Thailand). These twins, who were joined at the waist by a thin band of flesh, eventually settled down as farmers in North Carolina and married two sisters. Chang had six children and Eng had five children.

Signed, sealed and delivered

When is something 'signed, sealed and delivered'?

When it has been completed efficiently. This was originally a legal expression dating from when an important document was signed and sealed with sealing wax before being given to the recipient.

Silhouette

Where did we get the word 'silhouette'?

The term is derived from the name of the French Comptroller General in 1759, Etienne de Silhouette, who became famous for his economy measures. Under Silhouette, business and commerce were stripped of unnecessary detail – even paintings were reduced to mere outlines. In this spirit of economy, portraits in black and white outline became popular – and were named 'silhouettes' in honour of the financier whose economy had suggested them.

Silver spoon

Why do we say a child of the rich is 'born with a silver spoon in his mouth'?

Because it was once the custom for the godparents of a child to present it with a silver spoon at the christening. But a child born of wealthy parents did not have to wait until his christening to sup from silver – he was practically 'born with a silver spoon in his mouth'.

Simony

How did bribery come to be called 'simony'?

The term was first used in old English law to refer to procuring an appointment to an important church position in return for a bribe. This practice got its name from Simon Magus, who offered money to the apostles Peter and John in the hope of obtaining a position of prominence like theirs.

Sit above the salt

What is the reason we say a person of prominence 'sits above the salt'?

The expression originally meant to be placed at the table as an honoured guest – at least equal in rank to the lord of the manor. For, in Saxon times in England, the salt cellar was set as a dividing line at the table – to separate the people who used the salt as guests of the host, from the men of the household who worked for him and so earned the right to share the salt.

Sit on one's hands

Where did we get the expression 'sitting on his hands' to describe an unresponsive person?

From the theatre – where, if the audience 'sits on its hands', it obviously cannot applaud.

Skin of his teeth

Why do we say a person gets by 'by the skin of his teeth'?

The expression is a literal translation from the Hebrew text of the Book of Job. Since teeth have no skins, getting by 'by the skin of his teeth' is to get by with no margin at all.

Skinflint

Why do we call a stingy person a 'skinflint'?

Pieces of flint were once used to make fire. The rocks could be split into smaller and smaller pieces and each piece could be used for this purpose. A 'skinflint' was once one who, in trying to save a penny on flint, would split a piece down to its final layer or 'skin'.

Skullduggery

How did evil actions come to be called 'skullduggery'?

Grave robbing was once a common crime, and a grave robber was called a 'skull digger'. From this, any criminal activity – especially one practised at night – came to be called 'skulldigging' or 'skullduggery'.

Skylark

Where did we get the term 'skylarking' for having fun?

'Lark' is derived from the Anglo-Saxon *lac*, which means 'play' or 'fun'. 'Skylarking' comes from the sailors' custom of mounting the highest yards of sailing vessels – known as 'skyscrapers' – and then sliding down.

Slapstick
Why is rough, raucous comedy called 'slapstick' comedy?
It is named for a device used by low-grade comedians on the stage. Two pieces of wood are fastened together loosely so that when wielded as a club they make a loud whack! To produce laughter, the comedians spank each other with this device, which they call a 'slapstick'.

Sledgehammer to crack a nut
Where do we get the expression 'using a sledgehammer to crack a nut'?
Sledgehammers are very large, very powerful iron hammers, first used in England in the fifteenth century. The phrase describes using excessive means or force to solve a minor problem.

Slick as a whistle
Why do we use the word 'whistle' in the expression 'slick as a whistle'?
It's because it is 'slick' – that is, sleek – inside. Wind blown into a reed pipe is slowed up by the reed but a whistle has no obstruction at all.

Slush fund
How did a 'slush fund' get that name?
Aboard a sailing ship, 'slush' is waste fat from the galley used to grease the masts. All extra slush used to be the cook's perk – and he didn't have to account for the money he made from selling it. Likewise, a 'slush fund' is money that need not be accounted for – and often had better not be.

Sneeze at
Why do we say something worthwhile is 'not to be sneezed at'?
If a statement seems worthless, you may not bother to reply; you may merely make the sound of a sneeze – 'humph', as we might write it. Something worthwhile, however, is not to be sneezed at.

Snob
What is the origin of 'snob'?
The word comes from the Scottish *snab*, meaning 'boy' or 'servant'. All college students in England were at one time members of the nobility – and applied *snab* in the sense of 'servant' to the townsmen. The word '*snab*' was changed to 'snob' in the 1600s, when Cambridge University decided to admit 'commoners' as students. Cambridge required that such students, when registering, describe their social position with the Latin words *sine nobilitate*, meaning 'without nobility'. The students abbreviated this to *S. Nob*. When spoken, this abbreviation seemed so much like the word '*snab*' that it came to be written 'snob' and used to signify 'a pretender to position'.

Soap opera

Why is a television series of fictional lives a 'soap opera'?

In America, the early series of these kinds were sponsored first by soap powder manufacturers, then by other companies, who in return for the funding could advertise their products. This form of sponsorship was not allowed in Britain at that time. The word 'opera' was used ironically, the intellectual level of these series being well below that of grand opera.

Soft soap

What is the origin of the expression 'soft soap'?

The term was first used by confidence men as a synonym for flattery. Since soap that has become soft is extremely slippery, you used 'soft soap' to 'grease the skids' you put under a 'sucker'.

Soldier

How did the 'soldier' get his name?

The word comes from the Latin *solidus* – the name of a very valuable Roman gold coin. The Roman soldier worked for whichever master would pay him; he was a mercenary.

Spanner in the works

What do we mean by 'throw a spanner in the works'?

To cause mayhem, either deliberately or by accident. A spanner flung into the gears and pistons of an engine would inevitably create chaos.

Speakeasy

Where did we get 'speakeasy' as the name for an illicit saloon?

The term is Irish in origin. You couldn't raise your voice riotously or kick up a rumpus in an establishment where liquor was sold contrary to the Prohibition Law, without calling the attention of the police to the existence of the place. In order not to have the cops come and nab you, you had to 'speak easy'.

Spendthrift

What is the origin of the word 'spendthrift'?

A spendthrift is one who 'spends' the 'thrift' – that is, the savings – of another. The term was first applied to the young man who, upon inheriting his father's fortune, immediately spent it.

Sphinx

How did the Sphinx get its name?

The name is Greek and means 'the strangler'. The Sphinx got her name because, according to legend, she strangled the travellers who could not solve the riddle she propounded. Though the name is Greek, the legend is Egyptian; and though the sphinx of the legend is a woman, the famous Sphinx statue of Egypt bears the head of a man.

Spick and span

Why is something brand new or spotlessly clean called 'spick and span'?

In shipbuilding jargon, from the time when ships were built of wood, spick was a variant of 'spike' and span once meant 'chip'; a ship was 'spick and chip' new if leftover spikes and chips were still lying around. The Norse Word *span-nyr* means a chip of wood newly carved from timber, and from this it is easy to see how *span-new* emerged.

Spin doctor

What is a 'spin doctor'?

Someone who presents information in a particular way to elicit the reaction they want. The term originated in America in the 1980s and is usually used in a political context to mean someone with the talent – or cunning – to present a negative situation in a positive way.

Spitting image

Why do we call a very close resemblance 'the spitting image'?

The expression is a corruption of the earlier phrase, 'the very spit and image'. It referred to two people so similar that even their spit was alike. The change to 'spitting' came about from the general proclivity among boys, at least of an earlier generation, to try to spit like their fathers.

Splice the main brace

Where did we get the expression 'splice the main brace' for taking a drink?

The term is nautical and there's a certain amount of humour attached to it. Any 'brace' or rope that is worn can be strengthened by splicing (joining together). Similarly, a man is strengthened by strong drink – and so, to 'splice the main brace' is to serve out grog.

Spruce up

What is the origin of the expression 'spruce up'?

'Spruce' literally means 'like the Prussians', whose soldiers were famously elegant and tidy. It's from the French word for Prussia, *Prusse*. 'Spruce fir' is the Prussian fir tree; 'spruce beer' is beer made from the Prussian fir. And so, to 'spruce up' is to dress like a Prussian.

Stalking horse

Where did we get the name 'stalking horse' for a person used as a cover or decoy?

From hunting. One method of stalking game in an open field is to walk along hidden by your horse; a horse used in this manner is a 'stalking horse'. From this we get the name – and our present meaning of a person used to cover the true aims of an organisation or proceeding.

Stall off
Why do we say we 'stall off' an impending event?

A 'stall' is a decoy bird. From this, the person who assisted a pickpocket by diverting the attention of the victim came to be called a 'stall'. We use the term to mean 'playing for time', because the pickpocket's assistant's two chief duties are to distract attention and play for time.

Stamping ground
How did a common gathering place come to be called a 'stamping ground'?

The allusion is to the fact that deer and other animals often have special spots that they visit day after day. Since you can detect such a spot by observing the ground (it will be thoroughly churned up) it's called a 'stamping ground'.

Star chamber
Where did we get the expression 'star chamber proceedings'?

'Star chamber' as a name for a court of justice with strict arbitrary rules. The term comes from an ancient English high court of that name, noted for its random methods and rules. It was called the 'star chamber' because stars were painted on the ceiling of the chamber in which the judges met.

Starboard
What is the reason the right side of a ship is called 'starboard'?

The term comes from the Old English *steor-bord*, meaning 'steering side' – because all early sailing ships had the steering oar placed on the right side of the ship.

Steal one's thunder
Who first accused someone else of 'stealing his thunder'?

The playwright John Dennis, around the year 1700. Dennis said he had invented a machine that could produce the sound effect of thunder off stage and complained that his rivals had 'stolen his thunder'. The idea of stealing thunder so tickled the fancy of people that the phrase was adopted into the language.

Steeplechase
Why is a horse race over obstacles called a 'steeplechase'?

Fox hunting gave us the term. If during a hunt no fox was found or the fox got away, some member of the hunt was likely to say, 'I'll race you to the next town', and point to its most distinctive feature at a distance – the church steeple. The hunters would then start off, no longer on a fox chase, but on a 'steeple chase'. From this, any race that is run over barriers is called a 'steeplechase'.

Steward

How did a caretaker come to be called a 'steward'?

Originally the steward was employed to take care of pigs and cattle – because at one time these were the most important sources of wealth for the Saxon landlords. 'Steward' comes from the Anglo-Saxon word *stigweard* meaning 'sty-keeper'.

Stickler

Why is a fussy person called a 'stickler' for detail?

Because the Middle English word from which it's derived, *stightlen*, means 'to set in order'. Originally 'sticklers' were judges at duels, who saw to it that the rules of fair play were closely observed. Today, the 'stickler' still follows rules very closely; he or she allows no deviation whatsoever.

Sticky wicket

Why is a tricky situation a 'sticky wicket'?

A cricket pitch (or 'wicket') left uncovered during rain would be moist and sticky when play resumed, making it difficult or even dangerous to play on, as the bounce of the ball becomes unpredictable. A 'sticky wicket' in common usage is a situation that requires careful negotiation to get through successfully.

Stooge

What is the origin of the word 'stooge'?

'Stooge' was originally a theatrical term and was first used to designate a comedian's accomplice who would have been hidden in the audience. From the fact that his real identity and purpose were not known to the other members of the audience, he came to be called a 'stool pigeon' – which, by elision, became 'stooge'.

Stool pigeon

Where did the 'stool pigeon' get that name?

The original 'stool pigeons' were real pigeons seated on stools. They were used by pigeon hunters who, when they went out to net passenger pigeons for market, would tie a captive pigeon to a stool placed in front of the net. Then with strings attached to the stool pigeon's wings they'd make them flap – and so entice other pigeons into the net.

Strait-laced

Why is a priggish person called 'strait-laced'?

Because a person wearing a 'strait-laced' corset is hemmed in and cannot bend. 'Strait' is from the Latin *strictus*, meaning 'tight' or 'drawn close'.

Strike while the iron's hot
Does 'strike while the iron's hot' derive from a blacksmith's work?
Yes. The smith has to remove the metal from the fire and work at it with his hammer and anvil while it is still red hot and malleable. Our more general use of the term is that we should take action at the optimum time. 'Going at it hammer and tongs' and 'having other irons in the fire' also originated from the blacksmith's art. The former means to act with great force or violence: the latter that, while someone may be undertaking a particular course of action, he or she has taken care that there are other options.

Stroppy
When we call an irritable, argumentative person 'stroppy', does it refer to the leather and canvas straps traditional barbers use to sharpen their razors?
No. It's British slang dating from the 1950s, a loose abbreviation of 'obstreperous'. It's another of those adjectives that will be only too familiar to parents of a teenager. A regional variation is 'mardy'.

Stumbling block
Where do we get the term 'stumbling block'?
'Stumbling' comes from a tree stump, which might easily be tripped over. We use this to describe an obstacle that prevents the smooth conclusion of our plans.

Stumped
Why do we say a person who is unable to answer a question is 'stumped'?
When a person is 'stumped', he or she is outwitted; and in the game of cricket the bowler who has succeeded in hitting the wicket, or 'stump', has outwitted the batsman.

Sucker
How did a gullible person come to be called a 'sucker'?
A rather stupid fish is called a 'sucker' – because it sucks up its food. It will indiscriminately take in live food, garbage or a worm dangled in front of it on a hook. A person who, like the fish, complacently swallows the bait, is also a 'sucker'.

Sundae
When and where did the ice cream sundae get its name?
In the 1890s at E.C. Berners' ice-cream store in Two Rivers, Wisconsin. One night Berners sold a dish of vanilla ice cream to a boy named George Hallauer. George saw a bottle of chocolate syrup that was used for sodas and asked for some to be poured over his ice cream. Other customers tried the combination and liked it and soon it became so popular that it spread to other towns. The only drawback was the expense of selling both syrup and ice cream for only a nickel, so some ice-cream sellers decided to sell this dessert for a nickel only on Sundays – which is how it became known as a 'Sunday'. The change in the spelling of the word came about at a later date and was the invention of an unknown merchant who wished to make the concoction seem more elegant.

Supercilious
Why do we call a haughty person 'supercilious'?
Because in Latin *super* means 'above' and *cilium* means 'eyebrow'. A supercilious person goes about with raised eyebrows.

Sure as eggs are eggs
Why are eggs the epitome of certainty?
They're not. This saying is a deliberate joking corruption or a mishearing of 'x is x', an irrefutable proof in mathematical science.

Swab
What is the origin of 'swab' as a nickname for a seafaring man?
Washing down the decks of their vessels was once one of the major peacetime occupations of Navy men. To do this they used a mop or 'swab'. So the sailors were called 'swabs'. But the sailors did not apply this term to themselves; instead, observing the similarity in appearance between their mops and their officers' epaulettes, they called their officers 'swabs'.

Swashbuckler
How did a romantic hero come to be called a 'swashbuckler'?
A 'buckler' is a small shield and to 'swash' is to 'swish'. A swashbuckler 'swishes' his sword and rattles it on his shield or 'buckler'.

Swings and roundabouts
Why do we say two options are 'swings and roundabouts'?
The full saying is 'what you lose on the swings you gain on the roundabout'. It means that each of two possible choices has its advantages and disadvantages and neither outweighs the other.

Sword of Damocles
How did the expression 'sword of Damocles' come to represent impending danger?
It's an allusion to an ancient Greek legend. Dionysius the Elder was a clerk who seized the throne of Syracuse. Damocles was one of his courtiers who envied him his power and wealth. So Dionysius invited Damocles to share his luxurious life for an evening. The two sat down to a rich banquet – but over the head of Damocles there was hung a sword suspended by a single thread. When Damocles complained that he couldn't enjoy the food at all because he was so afraid the sword would fall, Dionysius said: 'Under such a threat do I enjoy my wealth and power.'

Table d'hôte

Why do we call a fixed-price meal a 'table d'hôte'?

The term is French and literally means 'table of the host'. During the Middle Ages, almost all public eating places were operated on what is now called the American plan. Guests sat at the 'table of the host', took whatever was offered, and had to pay for the entire meal no matter what they ate. So, 'table d'hôte' came to signify 'a complete meal at a fixed price'.

Take a back seat

Does 'take a back seat' have a motoring origin?

No. The term is applied to members of parliament with little influence who sit at the back of the House of Commons – on the 'back benches'. In wider use, those who 'take a back seat' have (or chose to have) little interest or involvement in what's going on around them.

Take the cake

Where did we get the expression 'that takes the cake'?

From the competitive cakewalk. This dance originated in the Southern United States – and got its name from the fact that at barbecues, picnics and box suppers a strutting contest was held among the men. The man who cut the best capers in 'strutting his stuff' was given his choice of cakes – and with the cake he also got the girl who had baked it as a partner for the meal.

Take an early bath

If someone is forced to stop an activity earlier than intended, why does he 'take an early bath'?

The bath here is the one taken at the conclusion of a sporting event, particularly a football or rugby match. This is usually a communal activity for the entire team, so someone taking an early bath has had to retire from the game sooner than he might have wanted or expected.

Take a gander
Why do we use the phrase 'take a gander' to mean take a look?
The month after a wife's confinement was once called the 'gander month' or 'gander moon' – in allusion to the aimless wandering of a gander while the goose sits on the eggs. During this period, the husband was called a 'gander mooner' – and pleaded a certain amount of indulgence in matters pertaining to sex. So, originally, to take a gander was to 'take a walk and give the girls the eye' as a gander mooner would do. The phrase as we use it today retains some of this meaning.

Take a tip
How did 'take a tip' come to mean 'take a hint'?
This tip is from 'tip off', which in turn comes from the expression 'tip the wink' – that is, tilt the eyelid a bit to give a hint.

Taken aback
Why do we say that a person who is surprised is 'taken aback'?
It's a nautical term. When the sails of a square-rigged sailing ship are suddenly carried by the wind back against the mast – as sometimes happens in a strong gale – the ship is 'taken aback' and stopped dead. So too, a person halted abruptly by some new development is taken aback.

Taking the piss
How did ridiculing someone come to be called 'taking the piss'?
From the early seventeenth to the mid-nineteenth centuries, human urine was a vital ingredient in the cloth-dying industry. Much of it was collected from buckets on street corners, particularly in London and Newcastle, and these buckets were emptied weekly into barrels and taken by land, then sea, to North Yorkshire for processing. As the cargo aged, the smell must have become appalling. A worker in this shameful transport would use all sorts of euphemisms rather than admit to what he really did for a living; but anyone suspecting the truth might ask if, really, he was 'taking the piss'.

Talking turkey
Why do we say that when a person gets to the point he's 'talking turkey'?
It's an allusion to an anecdote. A Native American and a white man went hunting and agreed that they would share the game equally. They bagged three crows and two wild turkeys. The white man divided their bag and gave his hunting companion the first bird – a crow. Then he took a turkey for himself, gave the Native American a crow, took the other turkey and gave the native American the last bird – a crow. When he objected, the white man pointed out that he had three birds to his two. To which the Native American replied: 'We stop talk birds; we now talk turkey.'

Tantalise
What is the origin of the word 'tantalise'?
The Lydian king Tantalus was a son of Zeus. He made the mistake of revealing the secrets of the Gods to the people on earth, and the additional mistake of bringing down from Olympus the food and drink of the Gods – nectar and ambrosia – and offering them to mortals. As punishment, he was condemned to stand in water up to his chin while right above his head hung a cluster of luscious grapes. When he got thirsty and stooped to drink, the water receded; when he became hungry and tried to taste the grapes they moved to just beyond his grasp. Thus he was 'tantalised', the term we use today to describe being kept in a torment of anticipation.

Tawdry
How did something cheap and gaudy come to be called 'tawdry'?
At the annual fair held in honour of St Audrey on the Isle of Ely a very cheap and gaudy lace was once sold; it was called 'St Audrey's lace'. Over time, the first two words were run together and became 'tawdry'.

Taxi
What is the reason a 'taxi' is called that?
The word originally referred to the meter carried by the cab. It was called a 'taximeter' because it measured the fare or 'tax' – and cabs equipped with them proudly boasted of the fact by painting the word 'taximeter' on their doors. This was soon shortened to 'taxi'.

Teetotaller
Where did we get the name 'teetotaller' for a total abstainer?
The word seems to have originated with the doubling of the 'T' for emphasis, but it came into widespread use through its association with a temperance campaign. Members of a temperance society pledged themselves to abstain from distilled spirits. A later pledge bound the signers to total abstinence. The two classes of signers were distinguished by the initials 'OP', standing for 'Old Pledge', and 'T' for 'Total Abstainer'. The movement took hold and spread throughout America and the British Isles – with men signing a 'T-Total' pledge.

Tell it to the marines
How did we get the saying 'tell it to the marines'?
It grew out of the deep contempt that sailors of the British Navy had for men of the marines – not the US variety, but a military unit from the days of King Charles II. Jealous of its seafaring traditions and expertise, the Naval sailors made the marines the target of ridicule, presenting them as inferior, gullible fools with no understanding of the sea. So 'tell it to the marines' means: 'I don't believe you – but someone less intelligent might.'

Terrier

Why is a 'terrier' called that?

Because the Latin word for 'earth' is *terra*. Therefore, the home of a fox or badger – being a hole in the earth – is a 'terrier'. Because of this, a dog trained to chase a fox or badger from its terrier is also called a terrier.

Thimble

How did the thimble get that name?

The thimble was at first worn on the thumb; and, since it's shaped like a bell, it was called a 'thumb-bell'.

Third degree

What is the origin of the term 'third degree'?

The term alludes to Freemasonry. In order to become a 'third degree' mason, a candidate must pass a simple test. But many years ago uninformed non-masons got the idea that this test was very difficult; they believed it to be a nerve-racking mental and physical ordeal. The misconception persisted and the term 'third degree' ultimately became synonymous with a severe questioning of a reluctant prisoner by the police.

Third World

Why are some developing nations called Third World countries?

The term became widely used during the Cold War to describe countries that were aligned with neither the West nor the Soviet Bloc. It is not a geographical description, but 'third' here is similar to the use of the word in 'third party insurance' – a country's circumstances are the result of the actions of others, not of its own.

Three sheets to the wind

Where does the phrase 'three sheets to the wind' come from?

From sailing. The sails of a ship are fastened at one bottom corner by a 'tack', which is more or less fixed, and at the other by a 'sheet' which can be unloosened. Most commercial sailing vessels have three sails, each with its separate sheet, and when one of these sheets becomes loose the sail flaps back and forth and is said to be 'in the wind'. If all three sheets are 'in the wind', the ship and sails move about to no purpose as the wind blows them. So, a person reeling drunkenly about is said to be 'three sheets to the wind'.

Throw in the sponge

How did the expression 'throw in the sponge' come to be used as an acknowledgement of defeat?

In the early days of boxing, a contestant's seconds would toss into the centre of the ring the 'sponge' with which they had wiped his face as a sign that their man could not continue and they admitted defeat. The practice is continued today – except that a towel is substituted for the sponge.

Thug
Why are criminals sometimes called 'thugs'?
The original 'thugs' were members of a professional gang of thieves and murderers in India who made a practice of strangling their victims. The word is from the Hindi *thag*, meaning a cheat or swindler.

Tickled to death
What is the origin of the expression 'tickled to death'?
Legend has it that there was an old form of Chinese torture in which the victim was literally tickled to death. If this was true, then it is presumably possible to so tickle the fancy of a person that he too will die.

Tip
Why do we call a gratuity a 'tip'?
Years ago in English inns and taverns, it was customary for the patrons to drop a coin for the benefit of the waiters into a box placed on the wall. On the box was a sign that said: 'To insure promptness'. Later just the initials of the phrase were put on the box – TIP.

Tip of the iceberg
What is something that is only the 'tip of the iceberg'?
It's the obvious part of an issue that is in reality much larger or more complex. The bulk of an iceberg is concealed beneath the water, with only the very tip showing.

Toady
What is the origin of the term 'toady'?
The original 'toady' was the magician's assistant who ate toads so that his master could demonstrate his magical healing powers – since at one time toads were considered poisonous. The other duties of the 'toad-eater' were very much like those of the yes-men of today – to prove the boss right – and so we got the word and its meaning.

Toast
How did the word 'toast' get into the expression 'drink a toast'?
The 'toast' was once in the glass. The custom was to place a small piece of toast in the bottom of the glass as a delicacy. Since in drinking to a person you drained your glass, you downed this bit of toast as well.

Tommy Atkins
Where did the British soldier get the name 'Tommy Atkins'?
'Thomas Atkins' was the specimen name used by the British Army in its official regulations of 1815. One sheet, for instance, was headed 'Description of Service of Thomas Atkins'; another, 'Clothing Account of Thomas Atkins'; and a bounty receipt was made out, 'Received, Thomas Atkins, His "X" Mark'.

Tommyrot
Why do we call something that's worthless 'tommyrot'?
The term comes from the use of 'tommy' to mean 'food'. Since loaves of bread were once distributed in England by charity on St Thomas' Day (21 December), this bread was called 'tommy'. Then, British soldiers began calling all their food 'tommy' because it was issued to them much as the bread was distributed. Perhaps this food wasn't very good to begin with; in any event it was worthless when rotten.

Touch and go
Why is a hazardous situation 'touch and go'?
In the days of sailing ships, goods and persons were often transferred between ships by bringing the two vessels so close together that they touched. This was a risky undertaking so, following a successful transfer, the ships would 'go' – separate – as quickly as possible.

Tout
What is the reason a race-track tipster is called a 'tout'?
The word 'tout' is a dialect form of 'toot' – from the Anglo-Saxon *totian*, meaning 'to stick out'. The first touts were men who stuck their heads out of their shops in search of business. Later, bookmakers employed touts to give people tips on the races – and then tell them where they could place their bets.

Trade winds
How did the 'trade winds' get that name?
This particular 'trade' comes from the Old German *trata*, which literally means 'track'. The 'trade winds' follow a uniform track.

Tram
Where did the British get the name 'tram' for a streetcar?
From the German *traam*, meaning 'the handle of a dung sledge or wheelbarrow'. The term was adopted by English miners for the vehicle they used for carrying ore. The first railways were built not in the streets but in the mines – where they were used to carry the miners' trams.

Tried in the balance
What is the origin of the expression 'tried in the balance and found wanting'?
The expression refers to the ancient Egyptian belief that the soul of the deceased was weighed and its weight determined the fate he would suffer.

Trousseau
Why do we call the clothes a bride takes on her honeymoon her 'trousseau'?
The term comes from the French *trusse*, which means 'little bundle'. In early times the trousseau was a small bundle of household items that the wife took with her to her new home; it was a kind of dowry.

True blue
What is the origin of the expression 'true blue'?
The term originally referred to the blue aprons and jackets once worn by butchers, which did not show blood stains. But it got its present meaning from the adoption of blue as the colour of the pro-Parliament Scottish Presbyterian Party of the seventeenth century – as distinct from the royal red.

Trump card
How did a special card or suit of cards come to be called 'trump'?
The word 'trump' is a corruption of 'triumph'. A trump card is a card that can 'triumph' – or win over – the other cards in a game by virtue of its special powers.

Tumbler
Why do we call certain drinking glasses 'tumblers'?
It is because at one time these drinking glasses really 'tumbled'. They were made with a pointed or curved base so that you could not set them down until you had drained them to the last drop.

Turkey
How did the Native American bird get the name 'turkey'?
Guinea hens and cocks were first imported into England from Africa by way of the Turkish dominions – and so were called 'Turkey' cocks and hens. When the American bird was introduced, it was confused with the African and given the same name. Then, when a distinction between the two birds was finally established and the names were differentiated, 'turkey' was wrongly retained for the American bird instead of the African.

Turn down
Why do we say something rejected has been 'turned down'?
The phrase is derived from the old custom of turning down an empty glass when no more drink is desired – but a more direct antecedent was the courting mirror used in colonial days. This was a small hand mirror used by bashful swains to help them propose. The young man would bring one to the home of his sweetheart and place it face upward on the table. This action informed the young lady that he wanted to marry her. If her answer to this proposal of marriage was yes, she would smile at his image in the mirror. But if it was no she would turn the mirror, and therefore, his image, face down.

Turn a hair
Where do we get the expression 'he didn't turn a hair'?
It comes from horse racing. A horse that wins a race effortlessly, without working up a sweat and roughing up its coat, is said to have won without 'turning a hair'.

Turncoat

Why is a traitor called a 'turncoat'?

In the days when feudal lords maintained their own armies, each lord had a special livery for his servants and swordsmen. When a man left one lord for the service of another, he literally turned his livery coat inside out so that he might not be mistaken for an enemy upon approaching the castle of his new master.

Turned tables

Why are do we say this when opponents' positions are reversed?

The allusion is to board games such as backgammon, where the boards are turned round between play so that a competitor plays from his or her opponent's previous position.

Turnpike

How did main highways in America get the name 'turnpikes'.

The name comes from the poles or bars – that is 'pikes' – that were once swung on a pivot across the roads and had to be turned before vehicles or horsemen could pass. They were set up to ensure the collection of tolls on the highways.

Tuxedo

Why do we call a man's evening jacket a 'tuxedo'?

Because it was first worn at Tuxedo Park in Orange County, New York. But, according to legend, this coat was devised by King Edward VII of England while he was still Prince of Wales. As a young man, Edward liked to play cards and would often sit all night at the table – where, being rather stout, his full-dress coat tails got in his way. So Edward had a coat made with the tails clipped off and that's how the tuxedo came into being.

Tycoon

How did a person of importance come to be called a 'tycoon'?

The name comes from the Japanese words *tai*, meaning 'great', and *kun*, meaning 'prince'. The Japanese have never used the word among themselves, however; they use it only when they are speaking to foreigners in an attempt to impress them with their own importance and the sovereignty of their ruler.

U-boat

Why do we call the German submarine a 'U-boat'?

Because the German name for a submarine is *unterseeboot* – so the 'U' stands for 'undersea'.

Umbrage

Why do we say a person who takes offence takes 'umbrage'?

The word 'umbrage' comes from the Latin *umbra*, meaning 'shadow'. A shadow is a 'dark picture' – a gloomy view, as it were – and a person who takes umbrage believes the worst.

Umpire

Where does the word 'umpire' come from?

From the Old French word *nompair*, meaning 'not paired'. The umpire of a game is the third or 'not paired' person called upon to decide between two contestants.

Uncle

Why do we call a pawnbroker 'uncle'?

As a humorous pun on the Latin word *uncus*, meaning 'hook'. At one time pledges of clothing were hung on a hook or *uncus* in the pawnbroker's shop; his shop was, therefore, called *uncus* – and it's but a short step from that to 'uncle'.

Uncle Sam
How did Uncle Sam get his name?
The original Uncle Sam – goatee beard, flowing hair, twinkling eyes and all – was Samuel Wilson, born in West Cambridge, Massachusetts. In time, he moved with his brother Ebenezer to Troy, New York, where they formed a partnership in the meat-packing business. The brothers were contracted to supply the Army with beef and pork during the War of 1812, and marked their shipping barrels 'US'. The soldiers jokingly called the meat 'Uncle Sam's' beef or pork – since these initials coincided with the name. A soldier drew a caricature of Wilson and labelled the picture 'Uncle Sam of the USA'. This picture was the original of the ones used to depict Uncle Sam today. The first Uncle Sam died in Troy on 31 July 1854, and lies beside his brother Ebenezer in the Miller plot at Oakwood Cemetery. A monument has been erected in Troy to his memory.

Under the weather
Why is a person who is ill 'under the weather'?
It is because the greenhorn aboard a ship who feels slightly seasick, seeks shelter from the wind by crouching down beside the bulwarks – 'under' their protection – on the 'weather' or windy side of the ship.

Up to scratch
Why do we say a person who meets our expectations comes 'up to scratch'?
The expression comes from prize fighting. At one time a line was scratched on the ground with the toe and the fighters had to come up to it to fight. But neither could go beyond it – so one who wished to default just failed to 'come up to the scratch'.

Up to snuff
Why do we use the phrase 'up to snuff' to mean up to par?
The expression was first used to describe a person's physical condition. One of the most sensitive of all our senses is that of smell – it's the one most easily upset by our general physical condition. So a person who said he was 'up to snuff' meant he was able to sniff or smell; in other words, he was in fine condition.

Upbraid
How did 'upbraid' come to mean 'rebuke'?
'Upbraid' comes from the Anglo-Saxon word, *upbregdan*, which means 'to draw up'. When you upbraid a person you remind him of proper behaviour and make him stick to the rules.

Upper crust
Why do we call high society the 'upper crust'?
Because the crust on a loaf of bread was long considered the best part, and the upper crust, or top crust, the best part of all. If high society is the best of all, then it's 'upper crust'.

Upset the apple cart

Why do we use the phrase 'upset the apple cart' to mean bring about disaster?

The apple cart referred to is the human body. Ever since Adam was banished from Eden, man has carried the apple (that is, original sin) within himself. So, to upset a man's apple cart, is to upset not only what he is trying to do, but the man himself.

Upstage

What do we do when we 'upstage' someone?

We manoeuvre ourselves into a position of importance, to the detriment of others. 'Upstage' is a theatrical term for the part of the stage furthest away from the audience (at one time stages sloped upwards slightly towards the back). An actor who addresses the rest of the cast from upstage forces them to turn to face him or her, putting them in a subordinate position with their backs to the audience. A culprit is considered to be self-important and guilty of theatrical bad manners.

Utopia

How did the ideal world come to be called 'Utopia'?

The term is a combination of the Greek *ou* and *tópos*, which literally translated, means 'not a place' – that is, nowhere. The word was devised by Sir Thomas More, whose *A Fruteful and Pleasaunt Worke of the Best State of a Publyque Weale, and of the Newe Yle called Utopia* was published in 1516.

Vandal

Why is a person who needlessly destroys property called a 'vandal'?
The term gets its meaning from a Teutonic tribe. In AD 455 Genseric and his Vandal hordes captured Rome and mutilated the public monuments of the city, with no regard to their worth or beauty.

Vaudeville

How did American variety shows get the name 'vaudeville'?
The word is French and comes from the phrase *'chanson du Vau de Vire'*, meaning 'a song of the Valley of Vire'. The Vire is a river in Normandy, and in the fifteenth century Olivier Basselin, a fuller of that region, composed a number of light satirical songs that became very popular.

Ventriloquism

How did we get the term 'ventriloquism' as a name for throwing the voice?
The word comes from Latin and literally means 'to speak from the belly' – *venter* meaning 'belly' and *loqui* meaning 'to speak'. The Romans thought that ventriloquists spoke by using the air in their stomachs.

Vestal virgin

Why do we call an extremely chaste young woman a 'vestal virgin'?
Because the maidens of Imperial Rome who served at the temple of the goddess Vesta, were required to be absolutely chaste and were therefore called 'vestal virgins'.

Vicar

Why do we use 'vicar' as a synonym for 'minister'?
The term comes from the Latin *vicarious*, meaning 'substitute'. The original idea behind its use was that the vicar 'substituted' for Christ in interpreting the words of God.

Villain

How did a 'villain' come to be called that?

In feudal times this term meant 'one attached to the villa' – that is, the manor house. The notion of wickedness grew out of the assumption on the part of the feudal lord of the manor that all servants were knaves.

Volume

Why is a book called a 'volume'?

Ancient books were written on sheets of paper that were fastened together lengthwise and rolled up like a window shade. 'Volume' is from the Latin *volvere*, meaning 'to roll up'.

Vote with your feet

What do we do when we 'vote with our feet'?

We express disapproval or lack of interest by simply getting up and walking out – presumably having decided that this is a better course of action than staying around to attempt to resolve the issue.

Wash one's hands of

Why do we speak of 'washing our hands' of an affair we don't wish to be connected with?

Because that's what Pontius Pilate did when he yielded to the people and condemned Jesus – although he had found Him not guilty. But the custom is far older; baptism is a 'washing away of sins' and so are many more primitive customs.

Wash out

How did 'wash out' come to mean a failure?

In the early nineteenth century, British soldiers learned marksmanship by shooting at iron targets. The marks, if they were not good enough, were painted out or whitewashed. Thus a 'wash out' came to mean a failure or disappointment.

Weasel words

Why do we call the words a person uses in an attempt to talk themselves out of a tricky situation 'weasel words'?

A weasel caught in a trap will try to squirm and wriggle its way out. 'Weasel words' are those used when trying to get out of a tight situation.

Weather eye

How did we come to use the expression 'keep your weather eye open' to mean look out for danger?

The 'weather eye' is the one that looks towards the wind – the direction, as all sailors know, from which a change in the weather will be indicated.

Wet blanket

Why do we call a person who doesn't enter into the spirit of a party a 'wet blanket'?

A wet blanket will smother a fire – and a person who can't have fun at a party will have a similar effect.

Whatever
When was 'whatever' first used as a conversational block?
There are sporadic instances documented from the 1960s, but the expression became rife towards the very end of the twentieth century. The person on the receiving end of this interjection (often the parent of a teenager) is left in the frustrating position of having nothing whatsoever left to say, because 'whatever' is just shorthand for 'say what you want, not listening, not listening'.

Whatever floats your boat
What is meant by 'whatever floats your boat'?
That whatever makes you happy, however bizarre, is okay. The phrase originated in America but has been eagerly adopted elsewhere.

Whipping boy
What is the origin of the term 'whipping boy' for someone who is punished for another's misdeeds?
When a king's son was bad he should, like any other boy, have been whipped. But because he was of royal blood he couldn't be – and so it was once the custom to keep about the court some other boy who could be whipped instead of the prince.

White elephant
How did an onerous burden that cannot be got rid of come to be called a 'white elephant'?
The allusion is to the story of an Eastern potentate who, when he wished to impoverish or destroy a courtier, presented him with one of the court's sacred white elephants. The courtier then had all the expense of caring for the animal but, since it was sacred, could not put it to work. The ultimate effect was to reduce the courtier to poverty.

White feather
Why do we speak of cowardice as 'showing the white feather'?
When gamecocks are crossbred, a different coloured feather – more often than not white – shows up in their tails. It is generally believed that any outside strain will lead to cowardice in a gamecock – and so an act of cowardice is called 'showing the white feather'.

Whole kit and caboodle
What the is the origin of the expression 'whole kit and caboodle'?
The Dutch word *boedel* means the 'effects' that a person owns. Robbers, especially housebreakers, adopted the term – calling whatever they stole 'boodle'. They carried their burglar's tools in a 'kit'. If they were able to enter a house, gather up everything valuable and make a clean escape, they said they had got away with 'kit and boodle'. In time, the phrase was shortened to 'caboodle' – the 'ca' standing for the 'kit'. Then the 'kit' was reintroduced into the phrase – probably for emphasis.

Wide berth
Why do we say we give a 'wide berth' to something we avoid?
It's because the spot where a ship lies at anchor is called its 'berth'. If it has been anchored so it can swing freely with the wind and the tide and with all other ships at a distance, it has been given, quite literally, a wide berth.

Wild-goose chase
How did a 'wild-goose chase' get that name?
A wild-goose chase was once a sort of game – a horse race in which the second and each succeeding horse had to follow the leader accurately and at definite intervals. Since the horses had to keep their positions like geese in flight, the chase was called a wild-goose chase; and as this was no race – for no one could win – the phrase was adopted to describe a person following a course that leads to no prize.

Win hands down
Where did we get the expression 'win hands down'?
From horse racing. A winning jockey who hasn't had to raise his hands to tighten the reins or wield the whip has won 'hands down'.

Wind up
Why do we say a frightened or alarmed person 'gets the wind up'?
The allusion is to a deer or other animal which will, if startled, raise its head to 'get the wind up' its nostrils in an attempt to determine by scent if a predator is approaching.

Windfall
How did a bit of unexpected good fortune come to be called a 'windfall'?
Certain members of the English nobility were forbidden by the tenure of their estates to fell any trees, all the timber being reserved for the use of the Royal Navy. They could, however, use any that were blown down by the wind – and so a 'windfall' was unexpected good luck.

Wing and a prayer
How do we succeed 'on a wing and a prayer'?
This phrase has a specific origin. During World War I an American pilot returned to base with a badly damaged wing. When asked by his colleagues how he had managed not to crash, he replied that he had been praying all the way. Another pilot said: 'A wing and a prayer brought you back.'

Wisdom teeth
Why are our 'wisdom teeth' called that?
Because people were once supposed to have reached the 'age of wisdom' when they cut these teeth. But some people never have any!

Worth his salt
How is someone 'worth his salt'?
This expression derives from the salt allowance given to Roman soldiers, from which we get the word 'salary'. A person worth his or her 'salt' is entitled to all they have.

Write like an angel
Why do say a person 'writes like an angel'?
Although to 'sing like an angel' refers to celestial song, to 'write like an angel' refers to Angelo Vergece, a native of Crete. In the sixteenth century he was employed by both Henri II and Francois I of France because of his beautiful handwriting.

Writing is on the wall
Where do we get the expression 'the writing is on the wall'?
It's a Biblical allusion. In Daniel 5, 'handwriting' appeared on the wall of Belshazzar's palace wall during a feast – *Mene, Mene, Tekel, Upharsin* ('it has been counted and counted, weighed and divided'). Daniel interpreted this to mean that Belshazzar's deeds had been weighed in the balance and found deficient, and that he would therefore lose his kingdom.

Xmas

Why is Christmas so often written 'Xmas'?

The 'X' in this case is the Greek letter *chi* – written X – and *chi* is the initial letter of the Greek word for 'Christ'.

X-ray

How did the 'X-ray' get that name?

It was first called the 'Roentgen ray' in honour of Wilhelm Roentgen, the scientist who discovered it. But he preferred to call it 'X-ray', because 'X' is the algebraic symbol for the unknown and at that time he did not understand the nature of this ray.

Yankee
What is the origin of the term 'Yankee'?

The word comes from a nickname for the Dutch, *Jan Kaas* ('John Cheese'), Holland having long been famous for its cheeses. In pirate days, English sailors adopted the term as a derisive name for the Dutch freebooters. In this sense it became familiar in New York. Then the Dutch settlers there – noting its unpleasant significance – began to apply it to the English settlers of Connecticut, because they believed the Connecticut English to be far more enterprising than ethical. The term spread to the other colonies – though at first it was almost always used to refer with dislike to the citizens of a colony further North. It still is in certain sections – often with a 'damn' placed before it.

Yummy mummy
What is a 'yummy mummy'?

A mother who, though past the first flush of youth, is nevertheless still attractive, especially to younger men – who would probably describe her as being 'hot'!

Zany

Where did a fool get the name 'zany'?

From the plays performed by the Italian *commedia dell' arte* – in which the servants acted as clowns and bore the name *zani*. The word 'zany' was first used in English to designate a comic performer attending on a clown – a 'stooge'.

Zest

Why does 'zest' mean 'enthusiasm'?

Because in its Greek form 'zest' meant a piece of orange or lemon peel. The addition of a slice of orange or lemon peel adds 'zest' to a drink or dish – and makes us more enthusiastic about it.